International Logistics Management & INCOTERMS 2020 Rules

Dr. Vijesh Jain

Global Management Consultant, Corporate trainer,
Ex Director, United World School of Business
Ex Dean, IILM Business School

ISBN: 9798879111699
Imprint: Independently published

DEDICATION

I wish to dedicate this book to my distinguished professors at IIFT, New Delhi, who so passionately taught me theoretical aspects of business management way back in 1980s. I also dedicate this book to my numerous B School students, corporate students who have so passionately attended my various Topics and workshops on especially the topics related to How to successfully carry out export business in last 20 years. I also wish to dedicate this book to my wife and children who supported me wholeheartedly and with contribution to write this book.

CONTENTS

ACKNOWLEDGMENTS

This text is a result of inputs provided by several experts in the field of exports and imports, from industry as well as from academic world. I specially thank *Shri Rakesh Roshan*, Professor and *Shri Amit Kumar Rajvanshi*, Chief Manager-Global Supply Chain, at *Dabur India* for showing the correct path for contents formation for this book through valuable discussions. I am also thankful to my student of International Business *Arshvardhar* for arranging the text in correct order and seeing that layout is correct. Finally I wish to acknowledge the frequent support of *Shri Anil Kumar, Dr. Mukesh Porwal, Prof Navneet Saxena* and *Prof. Deepak Tandon* for their support and constantly guiding me to fine tune the information provided in this book.

INTRODUCTION

Topics 1 and 2:

Greetings and welcome, esteemed readers, to the enlightening journey that lies within the pages of "International Logistics Management and INCOTERMS 2020 Rules." I am Dr. Vijesh Jain, and it is with great pleasure that I extend my warm invitation to embark on this comprehensive and unique book dedicated to the practical intricacies of international logistics management and the indispensable INCOTERMS 2020 Rules.

In the dynamic landscape of global business, the movement of goods, both within a country and across borders, holds paramount importance. This book is meticulously crafted to provide you with an in-depth understanding of logistics management, placing a special emphasis on the complexities and nuances associated with international logistics.

The primary objective is to equip you with the knowledge, methodologies, and essential concepts involved in the international movement of goods. While we may touch upon aspects of e-commerce retail logistics, our primary focus remains steadfast on the transport of goods across seas, through the air, and other modes of transportation crucial to international trade.

Let's delve into some intriguing facts about the international movement of goods. Ever wondered what products top the list as the most shipped internationally? Allow me to share some insights.

At the forefront are innovative DIY furniture products, revolutionizing the furniture business with their space-efficient packaging and creative designs. Electronics claim the second spot, driven by the vast scale of production required for items like laptops, mobile phones, and semiconductor products. The third most shipped items are clothes, encompassing ready-made garments, textiles, and household textiles. Finally, food items, especially processed foods, secure the fourth rank among the most shipped goods globally.

A staggering 90% of internationally shipped goods traverse the seas, a testament to the cost-effectiveness and efficiency of sea transportation. This intriguing revelation underscores the monumental role played by enormous ships capable of carrying goods to virtually any destination worldwide. In fact, 10% of the world's Gross Domestic Product (GDP) now floats on the sea.

Did you know that the ubiquitous barcodes, commonly seen on supermarket products, were originally introduced in the transportation industry before making their way into retail? The transportation sector, particularly sea transport, has witnessed a revolution with the advent of colossal ships capable of carrying up to 24,000 20-foot containers, each laden with almost 15 tons of cargo. The significance of these mammoth vessels cannot be overstated, contributing to the astonishing fact that around 10% of the world's GDP now traverses the seas.

As we embark on this journey together, I invite you to absorb the wealth of knowledge that awaits within the following pages. "International Logistics Management and INCOTERMS 2020 Rules" is more than a reference book; it is a gateway to mastering the intricacies of global trade and logistics in the ever-evolving landscape of international commerce. Welcome aboard!

Now that we have delved into fascinating facts about the international movement of goods, let's expand our understanding further. One crucial aspect that shapes global logistics is the man-made marvels – the Panama Canal and the Suez Canal. These waterways significantly reduce the distance ships travel, providing a shortcut that is crucial for efficient international trade. The maximum size of ships that can navigate through the Panama Canal is currently around 12,000 TEU (twenty-foot equivalent units), highlighting the immense scale of logistics support achievable through sea transport.

These channels are not static; they are being widened to accommodate even larger vessels, projecting a future where ships with capacities of up to 18,000 TEU may soon navigate through these artificial waterways. As these ships grow in size, logistics costs become more affordable, contributing to the ongoing evolution of the international trade landscape.

However, the present times are marked by challenges such as the Russia-Ukraine war and the global pandemic, causing turbulence in the container shipping industry. Container rates have surged, nearly doubling from the prices observed in normal circumstances. While these challenges might be temporary, they underscore the delicate balance that governs the world of international logistics, emphasizing the need for resilience and adaptability.

As we continue our exploration, it's fascinating to learn that approximately 8% of the world's Gross Domestic Product (GDP) is allocated to logistics costs. This encompasses both international and inland logistics, providing a comprehensive view of the significant investment dedicated to moving goods across the globe. With 835 active seaports and inland dry ports worldwide, these infrastructural hubs form the backbone of international logistics, facilitating the smooth movement of goods.

Shanghai Port in China stands as the largest seaport globally, a testament to the pivotal role played by certain regions in shaping the maritime landscape. These insights into global logistics expenditure and infrastructure set the stage for a deeper exploration of the key topics covered in our book, "International Logistics Management."

In this comprehensive journey, we will explore the concepts of international movement of goods, shedding light on intermodal and multimodal transportation. The modes of transportation, including sea, air, rail, road, inland waterways, and pipelines, will be dissected to provide a holistic understanding of their importance in international logistics.

The book will unravel the significance of unitization, pelletization, and containerization, innovations that have revolutionized international trade, drastically reducing the cost of moving goods. Export packing and packaging, labeling, markings, and the role of intermediaries in the logistics chain will be discussed, offering valuable insights into the intricate web that enables the seamless movement of goods.

We will also delve into legal, regulatory, and institutional frameworks governing international movement, exploring crucial documents such as bills of lading and air waybills. The intricate world of ocean and air freight rates, international cargo insurance, major shipping routes, and ports will be unfolded, providing a comprehensive grasp of the dynamics that govern logistics costs.

Moreover, we will examine the role of dry ports, inland container depots (ICDs), and container freight stations (CFS), key players in making multimodal transportation efficient and fast. Case studies will spotlight initiatives by governments to enhance logistics efficiency, and a focus on technology's role in reducing costs, improving customer experience, and ensuring security will round out the book.

In joining this book, you are not merely acquiring knowledge; you are stepping into a realm where the intricacies of international logistics and supply chain management are demystified. The book is not just a compendium of information but a guide that will equip you with the skills to navigate the complexities of global trade. Welcome to the enlightening world of "International Logistics Management and INCOTERMS 2020 Rules." Let us embark on this journey of discovery together.

Thank you very much.

Chapter 1: Significance, objectives, learning outcomes and references of this book

Topic 3:

Significance: The International Logistics Management (ILM) book holds immense significance, particularly when viewed in conjunction with related books such as International Trade Operations and Documentation and the forthcoming International Supply Chain Management book in the VJ Export Mastery series. These books collectively form a comprehensive educational package that equips learners with a deep understanding of the complexities within the global trade and logistics arena.

Impact and Demand: The ILM book opens avenues for employment opportunities in both operational and marketing domains across sea surface transportation, air transportation, warehousing, e-retail logistics (especially in e-commerce), and the freight forwarding industry. Its impact is global, offering learners worldwide the chance to tap into diverse employment opportunities in these crucial sectors.

Objectives:

Familiarization with International Logistics: Understand the nature, characteristics, functions, challenges, and processes of international logistics.

Exploration of Concepts: Comprehend essential concepts, such as multimodal modes of transportation in both domestic and international trade, to address the evolving needs of large countries like India, China, Mexico, and Brazil.

Understanding Contemporary Scenarios: Gain insights into the current market scenario worldwide, including regulatory frameworks in different countries. For instance, the book explores the regulatory landscape in India as a case study, drawing parallels with global logistics.

Learning Outcomes:

Logistics Concepts: Develop an understanding of logistics concepts within the current global market scenario.

Containerization: Grasp the intricacies of containerization, a revolutionary aspect that has transformed international transportation, making it more efficient and cost-effective.

Multimodal Mix Analysis: Acquire the ability to analyze the multimodal mix of transportation for enhanced business gains.

Document Examination: Develop skills to examine the required set of documents for transportation, including bills of lading, air waybills, and other relevant documents.

Evaluation of Regulatory Framework: Gain the ability to evaluate the current scenario, including the regulatory framework, of the international logistics industry.

References: The book encourages learners to explore various resources, including books and articles, to deepen their understanding. The attached resource section provides a comprehensive list of reading materials, books, and online resources to supplement the book content. Learners can delve into these references to enhance their knowledge and gain additional insights into the dynamic world of international logistics.

In conclusion, the International Logistics Management book offers a well-rounded educational experience, preparing learners for diverse employment opportunities and providing them with the knowledge and skills necessary to navigate the complexities of the global logistics landscape. As we progress through the sessions, the book promises to offer a deeper understanding of the critical aspects outlined in this introduction. Welcome to a journey of comprehensive learning in international logistics management!

Discussion Questions:

Significance of International Logistics:

How do you perceive the significance of the International Logistics Management book in the context of global trade and commerce?

In what ways do you believe this book complements other books in international trade and supply chain management?

Impact and Employment Opportunities:

Can you identify specific industries or sectors where the skills gained from this book could be most valuable?

How do you think the current challenges, such as the Russia-Ukraine war and the global pandemic, might affect employment opportunities in international logistics?

Objectives and Key Concepts:

From your understanding, what are the key objectives outlined for this book in terms of familiarization and exploration of logistics concepts?

How would you explain the importance of comprehending multimodal modes of transportation in the context of large countries like India or China?

Learning Outcomes:

In your opinion, which learning outcome of the book do you find most crucial for a professional in the field of international logistics?

How might understanding the regulatory framework in different countries enhance one's competence in international logistics?

Containerization Revolution:

Can you provide examples or instances where containerization has had a transformative impact on international transportation?

How has containerization contributed to making international transportation more efficient and cost-effective?

Global Regulatory Landscape:

What challenges might arise for businesses operating in multiple countries due to variations in international logistics regulatory frameworks?

How can a comprehensive understanding of the regulatory landscape contribute to effective international logistics management?

Learning Resources:

Which specific books or articles from the provided references are you most interested in exploring further?

How do you plan to utilize online resources to enhance your understanding of international logistics beyond the book material?

Future Trends and Technology:

In your opinion, what role do you foresee technology playing in the future of international logistics and supply chain management?

How might advancements in artificial intelligence and the Internet of Things impact the efficiency and effectiveness of international logistics operations?

Application of Knowledge:

Can you think of real-world scenarios where the skills and knowledge gained from this book would be directly applicable?

How would you apply the concepts learned in this book to improve the logistics efficiency of a business or industry?

Personal and Professional Development:

What personal or professional goals do you hope to achieve by completing the International Logistics Management book?

How do you envision this book contributing to your career growth and development in the field of international logistics?

Feel free to discuss these questions with your peers or reflect on them individually to deepen your understanding of the topics covered in the book.

Chapter 2: Takeoff chapter for the main theme of the book

Topics 4: The birth of an idea

Hello, and welcome back to the book.

In this takeoff session, we'll delve into essential aspects of the international logistics industry, shedding light on its characteristics, demands, and the critical role it plays in global commerce. Additionally, we'll explore the connection between this book and the broader landscape of international operations.

Factors Influencing International Logistics Demand: Understanding the dynamics of international logistics starts with recognizing the factors that impact its demand. The strength of demand is intricately linked with market conditions. For instance, the disruptions caused by the pandemic in 2020 and 2021 significantly altered the demand landscape. We observed a unique situation where essential goods continued to move, but the overall demand dwindled, affecting various elements of the logistics supply chain.

Price Sensitivity and Trade Transaction Costs: Price plays a pivotal role in determining the demand for international logistics services. Price-conscious markets evaluate not only freight rates but also the entire trade transaction cost. This comprehensive cost includes expenses associated with goods clearance, handling, insurance, and customs, among others. Minimizing trade transaction costs is a strategic imperative, influencing the choice of shipping lines, transportation modes, and the application of technology.

Dominance of Sea Transportation: Despite the various factors at play, sea transportation remains the dominant mode, accounting for approximately 90% of international goods movement. The economic viability of sea transport, facilitated by large vessels capable of carrying vast quantities, underscores its importance. While sea transportation may take longer, the cost-effectiveness and scale it achieves make it an indispensable part of the global logistics network.

Characteristics of International Logistics Management: Examining the characteristics of international logistics management reveals a high operational cost environment. Fuel, capital, and vessel costs contribute to the complexity of the industry. Despite these challenges, margins for shipping companies remain thin due to fierce competition. Talent scarcity further compounds the industry's challenges, creating a premium on individuals with comprehensive knowledge of international logistics.

Infrastructure Challenges and Multimodal Transportation: Infrastructure bottlenecks pose challenges within countries, impacting the efficiency of logistics operations. Developed countries often boast advanced logistics infrastructure, with almost 90% of cargo moving through multimodal transportation. However, in developing nations, this percentage is lower, indicating infrastructural gaps that hinder seamless international logistics.

Consolidation and Client Expectations: The competitive nature of the industry has led to frequent consolidation through mergers, acquisitions, and alliances. Companies like BW Shipping, formed through the merger of major players, illustrate this trend. Clients in the international logistics sector are discerning and demanding, expecting the industry to invest in cutting-edge technologies. Technologies such as sensors, the Internet of Things (IoT), and blockchain-based solutions are crucial for meeting client expectations.

Conclusion: In essence, international logistics is a dynamic and intricate industry, shaped by market forces, technology, and a constant quest for efficiency. As we proceed with this book, we will delve deeper into the intricacies of international logistics management, exploring concepts, challenges, and solutions that define this ever-evolving field.

Chapter 3 : Logistics Sector in India - Opening Case Study

Topic 5: Opening Case Study: Logistics Sector in India

Let's delve into a comprehensive case study that explores the intricate landscape of the logistics sector in India. India, a vast country with a burgeoning need for both inland and international logistics, finds its logistics industry at a crucial juncture—poised for growth but still in its infancy.

Current Landscape: As of now, India's logistics industry is on the cusp of development, with bold targets set by the government to elevate it to global standards by 2025. The overall logistics market in India is exhibiting robust growth, with a Compound Annual Growth Rate (CAGR) of approximately 12% in 2020, and this upward trajectory continues. The primary drivers of demand in India stem from manufacturing units, catering to nationwide distribution, the expansive retail sector, Fast-Moving Consumer Goods (FMCG) products, and the rapidly expanding e-commerce retail segment.

Challenges and Opportunities: Despite the promising growth, the logistics spending in India stands at around 14.4% of its GDP, significantly higher than the world average for developing countries, which is 8%. This indicates existing bottlenecks and challenges, necessitating substantial investment in infrastructure projects. The Indian government has undertaken ambitious initiatives, investing in projects aimed at addressing these challenges.

Market Segmentation: The domestic logistics market in India is prominently characterized by Third-Party Logistics (3PL), a market segment valued at approximately USD 300 billion in 2020. Breaking it down further, the growth rate for transportation is around 12%, while warehousing follows closely with a Compound Annual Growth Rate (CAGR) of 10%.

Government Initiatives: Key government initiatives, such as the introduction of the Goods and Services Tax (GST), have proven to be transformative milestones in the history of India's logistics industry. Despite facing the significant impact of the Covid-19 pandemic, the Indian government remains committed to substantial infrastructure projects. These projects include the development of ports, road connectivity enhancements, and the establishment of large logistics parks. Foreign Direct Investment (FDI) plays a pivotal role in fueling these capital-intensive projects. For instance, FDI in ports, allowing up to 100% investment through the automatic route, showcases the government's commitment to fostering international collaborations and investments.

Opportunities for Professionals: In tandem with these developments, there exists a pressing need for international logistics professionals in India. The shortage of skilled individuals in this sector further underlines the potential for growth and the opportunities available in the logistics industry.

As we unravel the intricacies of the logistics sector in India, we gain valuable insights into its challenges, growth trajectory, and the transformative role of government initiatives. This case study serves as a lens through which we explore the evolving landscape of international logistics in one of the world's most dynamic economies.

Topic 6: Contemporary scenario of logistics in India

In our exploration of the logistics landscape in India, it becomes evident that the nation's logistics ecosystem is intricately woven into its economic and strategic fabric. Let's delve into the key elements that define the contemporary scenario of international logistics and the logistics sector in India.

Government Initiatives and Policies: The Government of India, recognizing the pivotal role of logistics in the nation's growth story, has set forth a strategic program and mission called Atmanirbhar Bharat. This initiative underscores India's commitment to self-reliance and emphasizes the importance of domestic manufacturing. In the face of global challenges, such as the coronavirus pandemic and geopolitical tensions, countries like India are compelled to look inward and enhance their manufacturing capabilities for domestic consumption.

Economic Growth and Defense Strategy: The logistics sector in India is not merely a facilitator of economic activities; it plays a critical role in national defense and security. Recent events, including the border dispute with China, have underscored the strategic importance of the international logistics sector. India's focus on building a robust logistics infrastructure is intricately linked to its economic growth, defense preparedness, and leadership position in South Asia.

Export Competitiveness and Economic Development: The expert group on logistics has identified international logistics as instrumental in enhancing India's position in South Asia. Additionally, export competitiveness stands out as a major beneficiary of improved logistics infrastructure. The focus is on reducing overall logistics costs, making the movement of goods within and across borders more efficient. Despite India's economic potential, high logistics costs have been a challenge, affecting businesses and consumers alike.

Challenges and Urgent Need for Investment: In recent years, due attention to the logistics sector in India has been lacking, leading to the country spending a disproportionately high percentage of its GDP on logistics. Inefficiencies and high costs in the movement of goods have hampered businesses and impacted consumers. Recognizing the urgent need for fresh investment, both from the government and the private sector, India is formulating policies to attract domestic and foreign investments to expedite much-needed infrastructure projects.

International Rankings and Performance: Assessing India's standing on the global stage, the World Bank's Logistics Performance Index (LPI) reveals areas for improvement. As of 2018, India ranks 44, compared to China at 26, the United States at 14, Singapore at seven, and Germany at number one. This underscores the potential for India to enhance its logistics performance, especially considering its large economy.

Classifications of the Logistics Sector: The logistics sector in India can be broadly categorized into three major areas—transportation, distribution, and storage. Transportation demands efficient cargo movement at affordable prices, while distribution requires a network of distribution points aligned with transportation carriers. Equally crucial is the need for large storage facilities, facilitated by logistics parks and warehouses.

As India navigates the complexities of the international logistics landscape and strives for self-sufficiency, the focus on bolstering the logistics sector emerges as a linchpin for economic development, defense preparedness, and global competitiveness. The urgency for investment and policy reforms is a clarion call to unlock the vast potential inherent in India's logistics sector.

Topic 7: Recent Developments and Ongoing Challenges in India's Logistics Sector

The Government of India has embarked on a transformative journey to bolster the infrastructure for logistics, recognizing its vital role in economic growth and international trade. Various policy initiatives have been introduced to address the inefficiencies within the logistics sector and integrate the three major dimensions—transportation, distribution, and storage. Despite these commendable efforts, there are several challenges that continue to impede progress.

Challenges to Government Initiatives:

Poor Integration Across Networks:

An overarching challenge lies in the poor integration of transport networks, information technology, warehouses, and distribution facilities. A seamless, integrated approach is essential for optimizing the movement, distribution, and storage aspects of logistics.

Diverse Regulations Across Regions:

With India comprising 28 states and multiple union territories, the logistics sector grapples with diverse regulations and guidelines. Achieving synergy and establishing a unified regulatory mechanism across the nation is imperative for a streamlined logistics sector.

Untrained Manpower:

The shortage of skilled professionals in the logistics sector is a significant challenge. Efforts are underway to enhance education and training in this domain, crucial for addressing the complexities of modern logistics management.

Dominance of Unorganized Sector:

The majority of logistics sector entities operate in the unorganized sector, with small truckers often having fewer than 20 trucks. This unorganized structure hampers efficiency and inhibits the optimal execution of international logistics, contributing to higher overall logistics costs.

Inadequate Training Facilities:

The lack of professional training facilities for modern logistics management poses a hurdle. Strengthening training programs is crucial to equip the workforce with the skills needed to meet contemporary logistics challenges.

Poor Client Services:

The unorganized sector often provides subpar client services due to untrained personnel in marketing and operations. Ensuring better client services is vital for fostering sector growth and establishing a positive reputation.

Lack of Infrastructure:

The dearth of robust infrastructure remains a significant bottleneck. Adequate investment is required to build modern logistics hubs, warehouses, and distribution centers, especially in regions lacking in proper facilities.

Absence of Specialist Equipment:

The logistics sector in India faces challenges related to the absence of specialist equipment such as refrigerators, advanced goods handling equipment, and ERP systems. These modern tools can significantly enhance efficiency and reduce overall logistics time.

Limited Research and Studies:

There is a notable absence of comprehensive research and studies in the logistics sector. The lack of field studies and essential data hampers the identification of gaps, inefficiencies, and areas that require rectification.

While the Government of India's initiatives reflect a commitment to advancing the logistics sector, addressing these multifaceted challenges is imperative. A concerted effort involving policy reforms, investment, training, and research is crucial to realize the full potential of India's logistics ecosystem.

Topic 8: *Possible Solutions and Future Prospects for India's Logistics Sector*

In addressing the challenges faced by India's logistics sector, various solutions and policy initiatives are being implemented, signaling a shift towards a more robust and efficient logistics ecosystem. Additionally, future prospects present opportunities for the integration of advanced technologies and sustainable practices.

1. Infrastructure Development:

A paramount solution involves a substantial emphasis and investment in building world-class road infrastructure, integrated rail corridors, dedicated freight corridors, and modern cargo facilities at ports. Urgent action is required to meet the escalating demands of the logistics sector.

2. Logistics Parks and SEZs:

Government policy initiatives include the establishment of logistics parks with a status equivalent to special economic zones (SEZs). This encourages private initiatives to develop state-of-the-art logistics infrastructure. An example is the logistics park in Mundra by the Adani Group, which incorporates a special economic zone.

3. International Collaboration:

Openly welcoming foreign training and research institutions in logistics and supply chain management is crucial. Collaboration with international players and educators can address the shortage of training and professional knowledge in the sector.

4. Foreign Investment Encouragement:

The government encourages foreign investment in logistics infrastructure, modern processes, and technology. Foreign Direct Investment (FDI) is sought to facilitate the adoption of advanced machinery, mechanized handling of goods, and the overall modernization of logistics operations.

Immediate Solutions Requiring Attention:

1. Modern Storage Infrastructure:

Development of modern storage infrastructure for perishable products is essential. Allocating more land for warehousing and logistics facilities in major metros and industrial hubs is crucial to keep costs in check.

2. Research and Development:

Focusing on research and development in both imported and indigenous technologies is vital. This includes implementing automated and sophisticated solutions for distribution, transportation, and storage to enhance overall logistics efficiency.

Future Prospects:

1. Adoption of Emerging Technologies:

India has the potential to be an early adopter of emerging technologies such as blockchain, artificial intelligence, and smart supply chains. Integrating these technologies can improve operational efficiencies within the country and enhance India's competitiveness in the global market.

2. Foreign Direct Investment in Technology:

Encouraging foreign direct investment in new technologies within India is key. Embracing green logistics practices and climate-friendly logistics solutions can contribute to sustainable development.

3. Development of Reverse Logistics:

The focus should extend to the development of reverse logistics, including the proper disposal of environmentally unfriendly products. Both government and private initiatives need to address the challenges associated with reverse logistics efficiently.

As India charts its book in the logistics sector, a combination of strategic policy initiatives, international collaboration, and technological adoption holds the potential to transform the logistics landscape, making it more efficient, sustainable, and globally competitive.

Topic 9: Government of India's Initiatives in the Logistics Sector

Recent initiatives by the Government of India showcase a significant commitment to infrastructure development, particularly in the logistics sector. These initiatives aim to address the challenges and inefficiencies that have impacted the sector, making it a focal point for both government and private sector investments. Let's delve into some of the key initiatives:

Key infrastructure projects

INDIA LOGISTICS

Sl. no	Projects	Target completion
1	Western and eastern dedicated freight corridors	June 2022
2	Delhi Mumbai Expressway (DME)	March 2023
3	Sagarmal initiatives	Phase wise development till 2035
4	Delhi Mumbai Industrial Corridor	Cluster development approach over medium to long term
5	MMLP network under implementation	Medium to long term

Sagarmala Project:

The Sagarmala project is a comprehensive initiative focusing on the development of road and port infrastructure, logistics parks, and dedicated freight corridors. The project, expected to continue until 2035, has already witnessed substantial progress, with 80,000 crore rupees of the total investment of over 2.12 lakh crore rupees being spent.

Sagarmal initiative

Status of Sagarmala projects (FY20)
– under implementation projects to be completed phase wise by 2035

S. No	Project Theme	Total		Completed		Under Implementation	
		#	Project Cost (Rs. Cr)	#	Project Cost (Rs. Cr)	#	Project Cost (Rs. Cr
1	Port Modernization	206	78,611	81	24,113	59	24,288
2	Connectivity Enhancement	201	1,28,786	38	9,416	88	91,157
3	Port Led Industrialization	34	1,42,457	8	45,300	23	96,046
4	Coastal Community Development	59	5,300	16	1,403	20	954
	Total	**500**	**3,55,154**	**143**	**80,233**	**190**	**2,12,445**

190 projects (costing Rs. 2.12 Lac Crore) are in various stages of implementation

Source: Company website

Back

Bharatmala Project:

The Bharatmala project encompasses the development of multi-modal logistics parks (MMLPs) and aims to create an extensive network of 35 MMLPs across the country. These logistics parks are strategically located to enhance the efficiency of cargo movement and reduce logistics costs.

Dedicated Freight Corridors:

Western and Eastern dedicated freight corridors are vital infrastructure projects in progress. With a target completion date in 2022, these corridors are designed to facilitate the seamless movement of cargo by rail across the vast expanse of India.

Dedicated freight corridor – Western and Eastern freight corridor

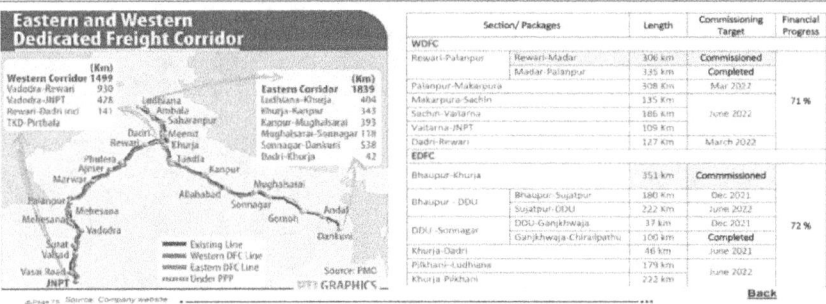

Back

Delhi-Mumbai Expressway (DME):

The Delhi-Mumbai Expressway is a major infrastructure project with a target completion date set for 2023. Spanning 1350 km, this eight-lane expressway is expected to significantly reduce travel time between Delhi and Mumbai, crucial for efficient connectivity to the major international seaport in Mumbai.

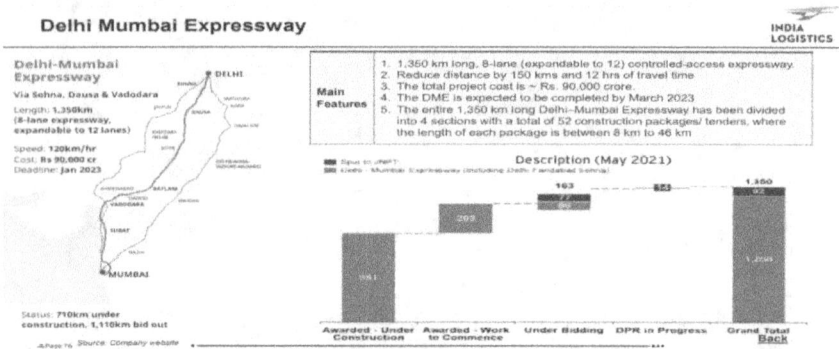

Delhi-Mumbai Industrial Corridor (DMIC):

The DMIC involves cluster development along the route between Delhi and Mumbai. Identified clusters in Rajasthan, Gujarat, and other states aim to boost industrial activities, creating economic opportunities and improving connectivity.

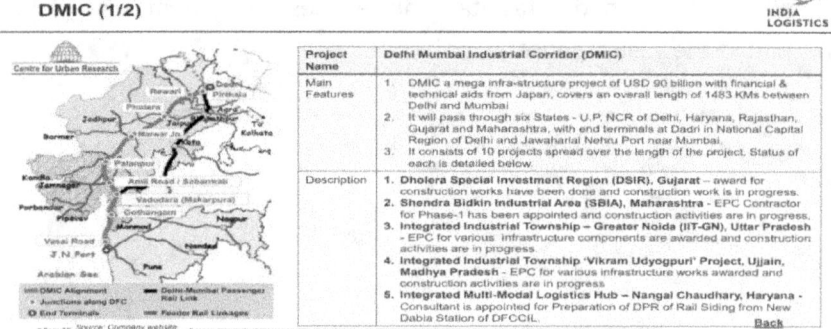

DMIC (2/2)

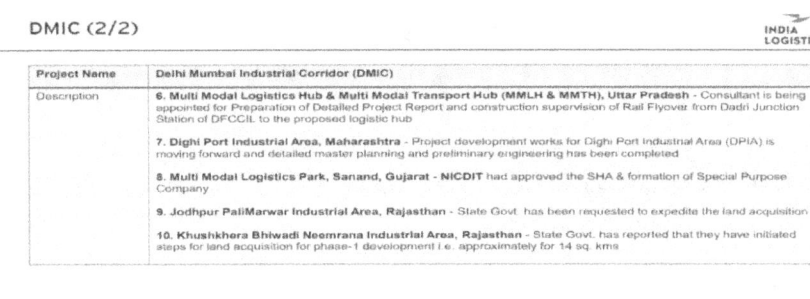

Project Name	Delhi Mumbai Industrial Corridor (DMIC)
Description	6. Multi Modal Logistics Hub & Multi Modal Transport Hub (MMLH & MMTH), Uttar Pradesh - Consultant is being appointed for Preparation of Detailed Project Report and construction supervision of Rail Flyover from Dadri Junction Station of DFCCIL to the proposed logistic hub
	7. Dighi Port Industrial Area, Maharashtra - Project development works for Dighi Port Industrial Area (DPIA) is moving forward and detailed master planning and preliminary engineering has been completed
	8. Multi Modal Logistics Park, Sanand, Gujarat - NICDIT had approved the SHA & formation of Special Purpose Company
	9. Jodhpur PaliMarwar Industrial Area, Rajasthan - State Govt. has been requested to expedite the land acquisition
	10. Khushkhera Bhiwadi Neemrana Industrial Area, Rajasthan - State Govt. has reported that they have initiated steps for land acquisition for phase-1 development i.e. approximately for 14 sq. kms

Back

Multi-Modal Logistics Parks (MMLPs):

MMLPs are integral to the Bharatmala program, contributing to the containerization of domestic cargo movement. These logistics parks, distributed strategically across the country, are poised to enhance the efficiency of cargo handling and transportation.

MMLP network under implementation

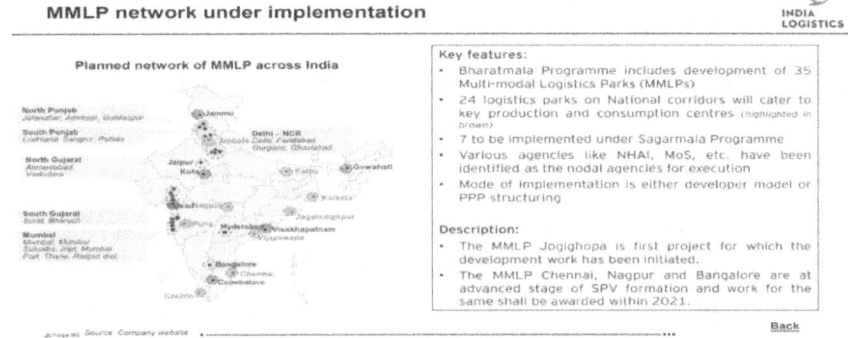

Planned network of MMLP across India

Key features:
- Bharatmala Programme includes development of 35 Multi-modal Logistics Parks (MMLPs)
- 24 logistics parks on National corridors will cater to key production and consumption centres *(highlighted in brown)*
- 7 to be implemented under Sagarmala Programme
- Various agencies like NHAI, MoS, etc. have been identified as the nodal agencies for execution
- Mode of implementation is either developer model or PPP structuring

Description:
- The MMLP Jogighopa is first project for which the development work has been initiated.
- The MMLP Chennai, Nagpur and Bangalore are at advanced stage of SPV formation and work for the same shall be awarded within 2021.

Back

Source: Company website

Regulatory Reforms:

Government-led regulatory and process-related reforms have played a crucial role in improving the efficiency of the logistics sector. Initiatives such as paperless exim trade processes, faceless assessment through Turant Customs, and the introduction of mandatory electronic toll collection systems like FASTag have contributed to streamlined operations.

Logistics Ease Across Different States (LEADS) Index:

The LEADS Index, introduced in 2021, provides a competitive benchmark among states and union territories in terms of logistics performance. States like Gujarat, Haryana, and Punjab have emerged as top performers in this index.

Target for Logistics Cost Reduction:

With a target to reduce the logistics cost from over 14% of GDP to less than 9% by 2025, the government is actively working on various fronts to improve efficiency, infrastructure, and overall logistics management.

These initiatives collectively represent a concerted effort by the Government of India to transform the logistics sector, making it more competitive, efficient, and aligned with global standards. The projects not only focus on immediate needs but also aim to create a sustainable and integrated logistics ecosystem for the future.

Topic 10: Key Takeaways from the Logistics Sector Case Study in India:

Enormous Growth Potential:

The case study underscores that India's logistics sector holds significant potential for growth. Despite being a large country with substantial logistics requirements, the sector is still at a stage of development where immense opportunities exist for expansion.

High Logistics Costs:

The logistics cost in India is relatively high, constituting approximately 14.4% of the GDP, compared to the world average of 8% for developing countries. This high cost indicates the presence of inefficiencies and bottlenecks in the logistics processes, requiring strategic interventions.

Low Containerization Levels:

The containerization of domestic cargo in India is only around 50%, considerably lower than the global average of over 90% for industrialized countries. This suggests a significant scope for improvement and modernization in cargo movement, especially for reducing costs and enhancing efficiency.

Government Initiatives and Investments:

The Government of India has launched several ambitious initiatives and infrastructure projects to address the challenges within the logistics sector. Projects like Sagarmala, Bharatmala, dedicated freight corridors, and the Delhi-Mumbai Expressway reflect a proactive approach towards modernizing and streamlining logistics operations.

Multi-Modal Logistics Parks (MMLPs):

The emphasis on developing Multi-Modal Logistics Parks (MMLPs) across the country is a crucial step. These logistics parks play a key role in integrating various transportation modes and optimizing the movement of goods, contributing to the reduction of overall logistics costs.

Regulatory Reforms and Efficiency Measures:

The government's focus on regulatory and process-related reforms, including paperless exim trade processes, faceless assessment, and the introduction of technologies like FASTag, highlights a commitment to improving the efficiency of logistics operations.

Competitive Benchmarking with LEADS Index:

The introduction of the Logistics Ease Across Different States (LEADS) Index provides a competitive benchmark among states and union territories. This initiative encourages healthy competition, fosters improvement, and enables a comparative analysis of logistics performance.

Optimistic Future Scenario:

With the ongoing initiatives, investments, and impressive progress, the case study suggests that India is at the cusp of a logistics revolution. The country is poised to join the league of the most efficient logistics industries globally, indicating an optimistic future for the logistics sector.

Need for Continued Focus and Participation:

The case study implies that sustained efforts, both from the government and private sectors, are crucial for achieving the desired transformation in India's logistics sector. Full participation, continued investments, and strategic planning will be essential to overcome existing challenges and fully realize the growth potential.

In summary, the logistics sector in India is undergoing a transformative phase, marked by government initiatives, infrastructure projects, and a growing awareness of the need for efficiency and cost optimization. The key takeaways highlight the opportunities for growth, the challenges to be addressed, and the positive trajectory towards a more robust and competitive logistics ecosystem in India.

Topic 10: Discussion Questions On the Case study

Logistics Cost Analysis:

How can India effectively reduce its logistics costs from the current 14.4% of GDP to the targeted less than 9% by 2025? What specific measures can be taken to address the existing inefficiencies and bottlenecks in the logistics processes?

Containerization Strategies:

Given the low containerization levels in India compared to global averages, what strategies can be employed to encourage higher rates of containerized movement for domestic cargo? How can the adoption of containerization positively impact logistics efficiency?

Government Initiatives Impact:

To what extent have government initiatives like Sagarmala, Bharatmala, and dedicated freight corridors contributed to the growth and modernization of India's logistics sector? What are the challenges and opportunities associated with the implementation of these initiatives?

Role of Multi-Modal Logistics Parks (MMLPs):

How do Multi-Modal Logistics Parks contribute to the optimization of logistics operations? What benefits do these parks bring to the movement of goods, and how can their development be accelerated for maximum impact?

Regulatory Reforms and Technology Integration:

What role do regulatory reforms and technological advancements play in enhancing the efficiency of logistics operations, as seen in initiatives like paperless exim trade processes and FASTag implementation? How can further technology integration improve overall logistics performance?

LEADS Index and State Competitiveness:

How effective is the Logistics Ease Across Different States (LEADS) Index in promoting competitiveness among states and union territories? What factors contribute to the success or challenges faced by states in improving their logistics performance?

Investment Opportunities and Challenges:

What are the potential investment opportunities in India's logistics sector, and how can both domestic and international investors actively participate? What challenges might investors face, and how can these challenges be mitigated?

Environmental and Sustainable Logistics:

How can emerging technologies like blockchain, artificial intelligence, and smart supply chains be leveraged to create more sustainable and environmentally friendly logistics practices? What role can the logistics sector play in addressing environmental concerns?

Skilled Workforce and Training Programs:

What steps can be taken to address the shortage of skilled manpower in the logistics sector in India? How can training programs and educational initiatives be improved to meet the demands of modern logistics management?

Global Benchmarking and Competitiveness:

How does India compare globally in terms of logistics performance, and what strategies can be implemented to improve its ranking on international indices like the Logistics Performance Index (LPI)? What can be learned from the logistics practices of top-performing countries?

These discussion questions aim to delve deeper into various aspects of the case study, encouraging a comprehensive analysis of the challenges, opportunities, and future prospects for India's logistics sector.

Chapter 4 : Understanding International Logistics.

Topic 13: Chapter Introduction: Understanding International Logistics

Friends, welcome to the inaugural session of our book on International Logistics Management. As we embark on this learning journey, we aim to delve into the intricacies of international logistics, exploring its scope, impact, and crucial role in the ever-evolving landscape of global trade.

In this section, we will navigate through various dimensions of international logistics, building upon the foundational concepts discussed in earlier sessions. Our primary focus will be to understand the breadth of logistics and identify its components that contribute to the efficient movement of goods on a global scale.

Key Topics Covered in this Chapter:

Scope of Logistics:

We will revisit the fundamental elements of logistics, expanding on the scope to encompass the broader international context. This exploration will shed light on the comprehensive nature of logistics management.

International Trade and Logistics Growth:

An exploration into the symbiotic relationship between international trade and logistics. We will analyze how the growth of one influences the other, examining the reciprocal impact of logistics efficiency on international trade and vice versa.

Objectives and Importance of Logistics in International Trade:

Unpacking the core objectives and significance of logistics in the realm of international trade. This section aims to underscore the pivotal role logistics plays in facilitating cross-border commerce.

Insights on Logistic Cost:

A detailed discussion on the intricacies of logistic costs, addressing how these costs can be optimized to enhance the overall efficiency of international logistics operations.

Objectives of Logistics Management:

Understanding the fundamental goals of logistics management, emphasizing the strategic and operational objectives that organizations aim to achieve through effective logistics practices.

Impact of Logistics on the Environment:

Exploring the environmental implications of logistics activities and introducing the concept of green logistics. This section delves into the growing importance of sustainable practices in the logistics industry.

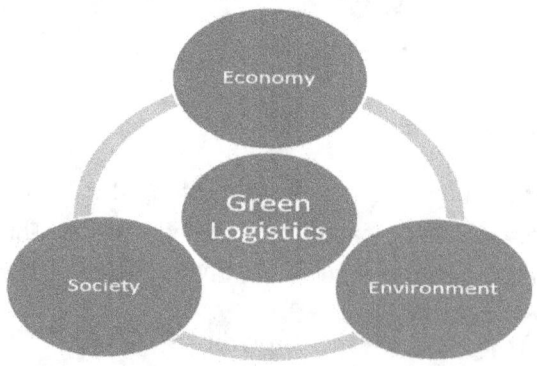

Value Chain in Logistics:

Unraveling the concept of the value chain within the logistics context. We will examine how different stages of the logistics process contribute to creating and delivering value to end consumers.

As we embark on this exploration, our goal is to provide you with a comprehensive understanding of international logistics, equipping you with the knowledge and insights needed to navigate the complexities of a globally interconnected supply chain. So, without further ado, let's delve into the world of Understanding International Logistics.

Topic 14: Scope of Logistics Management in International Trade

In the dynamic landscape of international trade, the scope of logistics management is experiencing a significant expansion. This growth is intricately linked to the ever-increasing complexities and demands of global commerce. As international trade flourishes, the functions and importance of international logistics management witness a parallel surge, creating a mutually reinforcing relationship.

Key Areas within the Scope of International Logistics Management:

Forecasting Customer Demands:

The ability to predict and adapt to customer demands on a global scale, considering geopolitical events and shifts in demand patterns among countries.

Strengthening Communication Channels:

Ensuring robust and efficient communication across international operations, involving various stakeholders such as buyers, sellers, logistics operators, and authorities. Emphasis on electronic data interfaces for streamlined communication.

Maintaining Distribution Channels:

Supporting and optimizing distribution channels, a critical element of marketing. This involves ensuring goods reach the right place at the right time, in the right quantity and at the right price.

Inventory Management and Control:

Efficiently managing and controlling inventory throughout the international movement of goods. This includes predicting, providing, and strategically placing inventories at crucial points to avoid unnecessary costs.

Handling Materials Requirements:

Ensuring the timely availability and movement of materials required for the international movement of goods, including raw materials and packing materials. Emphasizing just-in-time delivery to manufacturing units.

Processing Orders Efficiently:

Exploring the potential for logistics providers to take up the responsibility of efficiently processing orders from international clients. This includes managing large and varied orders, enhancing the third-party logistics environment.

Selecting Locations for Plants and Warehouses:

Contributing to forward and backward integration by assisting in the selection of optimal locations for manufacturing plants and warehouses globally. This involves strategic placement for efficient supply chain management.

Procurement of Raw Materials:

Evaluating the possibility of third-party logistics providers aiding in the procurement of raw materials at the right locations, thereby enhancing value for manufacturers.

Regulating Traffic and Transportation:

Managing and regulating the movement of goods in traffic, whether through charter ships or liner ships. Ensuring a smooth flow of goods in the most efficient manner.

Creating Time and Place Utilities:

Providing value for time and place utilities by ensuring not only the right place but also the right time and quantity of goods, contributing to the overall efficiency of the supply chain.

Movement Consolidation:

Offering consolidation services at various levels, including less-than-container load and full container load concepts. Consolidating clients with smaller quantity requirements to minimize transportation costs.

Handling Reverse Logistics:

Addressing the complexities of reverse logistics, including returns and other reverse processes. Alleviating the challenges companies face in managing reverse logistics.

Maintaining Customer Service and Support:

Integrating customer service and support functions to provide comprehensive post-sale services. Minimizing overall operational costs and ensuring a holistic end-to-end logistics solution.

In essence, the scope of international logistics management extends beyond conventional transportation and warehousing. It encompasses a spectrum of functions crucial for the seamless and efficient movement of goods in a globally interconnected supply chain. This book aims to provide a thorough understanding of these diverse aspects within the realm of international logistics management.

Topic 15: The Remarkable Growth of International Trade

In the backdrop of the longest peace time experienced by humanity post-World War II, there has been a remarkable surge in global economic activities and, more notably, in international trade. This era of extended peace, until recent geopolitical events, provided an invaluable opportunity to focus on enhancing globalization, liberalization, and privatization efforts worldwide.

Key Factors Driving the Growth of International Trade:

Advancements in Technology:

Significant strides in technology have revolutionized international trade by enabling the movement of larger consignments. This technological progress has, in turn, contributed to the reduction of transportation costs and associated trade transaction costs.

Reduction in Trade Barriers:

Concerted global efforts, spearheaded by institutions like the World Trade Organization (WTO), aimed at diminishing trade barriers. The WTO's role in advocating for fair and free international trade has led to a substantial decrease in both visible and non-visible obstacles.

Impact on Trade Transaction Costs:

The reduction in trade barriers, particularly tariffs, has visibly decreased trade transaction costs. This overarching achievement is attributed to the collaborative efforts of the international community in fostering a more open and interconnected global trade environment.

Global Technological Integration:

Integration of technology on a global scale has facilitated seamless communication, efficient supply chain management, and streamlined international trade operations. This interconnectedness has played a pivotal role in the growth of cross-border trade.

Emergence of LPG Policies:

The adoption of Liberalization, Privatization, and Globalization (LPG) policies by emerging markets and developing countries has been a game-changer. These policy shifts have not only benefited the economies of individual nations but have also significantly contributed to the expansion of international trade.

The Role of LPG Policies:

Privatization: Opening up sectors to private enterprises has led to increased efficiency, innovation, and competition, fostering a conducive environment for international trade.

Liberalization: Easing restrictions on trade and investment has facilitated smoother cross-border transactions and created opportunities for businesses to explore global markets.

Globalization: The interconnectedness of economies has reached unprecedented levels, creating a vast network for international trade to thrive.

As a result of these collective efforts, the world has witnessed substantial growth in both the global economy and international trade. While challenges persist, the reduction in trade barriers and the fostering of a more open trade environment have undoubtedly propelled international trade to new heights. The enduring legacy of the longest peace time has been the creation of a foundation for sustained global economic progress and interconnectedness.

Topic 16: Objectives and Significance of Logistics in International Trade

The fundamental objective of logistics in the realm of international trade revolves around ensuring the seamless flow of goods and services from the seller to the buyer across borders. The intricacies involved in achieving this objective are multifaceted, encompassing several key elements that directly influence the overall success of international trade transactions.

Core Objectives of Logistics in International Trade:

Ensured Flow of Goods and Services:

The primary goal is to guarantee the uninterrupted movement of goods and services across international borders. This involves meticulous planning and execution to overcome the challenges associated with cross-border logistics.

Right Products, Quantities, and Assortments:

Logistics aims to deliver the precise products, quantities, and assortments specified in the international trade agreements. Accuracy in fulfilling these requirements is crucial for meeting buyer expectations.

Timely Availability:

Time sensitivity is paramount in international trade. Logistics endeavors to ensure that goods are available at the right place and right time, aligning with the agreed-upon timelines and schedules.

Cost-Effective Movement:

Controlling the cost of transporting goods is a critical aspect of logistics. Efficient planning and utilization of transportation resources contribute to cost-effective movement, directly impacting the overall expenses associated with international trade.

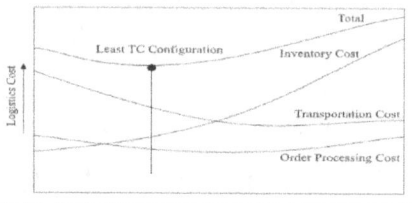

Fig. 1.1   Trade-offs between transport costs and inventory costs.

Spectrum of Logistics System Alternatives		
Few warehouses, premium transport, High Speed Order Processing	← →	Many Warehouses, Low-Cost Transport, Mail Speed Order Processing

Final Price Considerations:

Logistics plays a pivotal role in determining the final price of goods reaching the buyer. By optimizing the cost elements involved in the supply chain, logistics contributes to maintaining a competitive and justifiable final price.

Preserving Product Conditions:

Ensuring that goods reach their destination in optimal condition is a vital objective. Logistics strategies include measures to preserve the quality, integrity, and condition of the products throughout the journey.

Adherence to Terms and Conditions:

Logistics professionals work towards meeting the specified terms and conditions outlined in international trade agreements. This involves managing documentation, customs procedures, and compliance with trade regulations.

Significance of Logistics in International Trade:

Direct Impact on Cost:

The efficiency of logistics operations has a direct bearing on the overall cost structure of international trade. Cost-effective logistics contribute to enhanced competitiveness and profitability.

Buyer Satisfaction:

Logistics is instrumental in ensuring that the buyer receives the goods as per expectations. Timely delivery, product quality, and adherence to terms significantly contribute to buyer satisfaction.

Availability of Goods:

By orchestrating the timely movement of goods, logistics facilitates the availability of products at the right place and right quantity, meeting market demands effectively.

Global Market Competence:

Effective logistics management enhances a nation's or business's competence in the global market. Streamlined supply chains and reliable logistics operations contribute to market presence and competitiveness.

In essence, the objectives and importance of logistics in international trade are intertwined with the core principles of delivering value, meeting expectations, and optimizing the entire supply chain. As an indispensable component, logistics acts as a catalyst for the smooth and efficient execution of international trade transactions, fostering economic growth and global market integration.

Topic 17: Insights into Logistics Costs and Trade Transaction Efficiency

Understanding the overall logistics cost and trade transaction efficiency involves delving into the intricacies of international trade. The concept of trade transaction costs, representing the difference between the ex-factory price and the landed cost, is crucial in comprehending the challenges and optimizations in global trade.

Trade Transaction Costs and Global Trade:

Evolution in Reducing Transaction Costs:

Over time, humans have devised ways to mitigate transaction costs, enabling international trade to flourish. Despite examples of countries like India spending significantly on logistics, the business remains viable due to continuous efforts in reducing trade transaction costs.

Total Logistics Cost Perspective:

Adopting a total logistics cost perspective requires understanding the trade-offs between various cost elements. This involves a delicate balance, as reducing one cost may lead to an increase in another. The use of Information and Communication Technology (ICT) and digitalization plays a pivotal role in finding optimal trade-offs.

Role of Digitalization and ICT:

Leveraging digitalized systems, such as Enterprise Resource Planning (ERP) and emerging technologies like the Internet of Things (IoT) and smart sensors, facilitates the identification of trade-offs in a complex total cost perspective. Digitalization enables a more efficient and optimized approach to logistics management.

New Technologies Shaping Insights:

Advancements in digital technologies, including IoT, smart logistics, and the upcoming concepts of Non-Fungible Tokens (NFTs) and the metaverse, are transforming the way insights into logistics costs are gained. These technologies offer new avenues for improving trade transaction efficiency.

Insights from a Total Logistics Cost Perspective:

Understanding Trade-Offs:

Trade-offs are inherent in logistics management, especially concerning inventory cost, transportation cost, and order processing cost. A graphical representation of these trade-offs, facilitated by digital means, aids in optimizing overall trade transaction costs.

Spectrum of Costs:

Costs vary across a spectrum, ranging from few warehouses, premium transport, and high-speed order processing to many warehouses, low-cost transport, and slower order processing. Finding the right trade-off within this spectrum is critical for cost reduction.

Digital Technologies as Enablers:

Digital technologies provide a broad spectrum of costs in the logistics chain. Efficient digital solutions help in plotting and analyzing trade-offs, contributing to the reduction of overall trade transaction costs.

Beyond Logistics: Trade Transaction Costs from a Marketing Perspective:

Complexity in Marketing Chain Costs:

Expanding the perspective to include marketing costs introduces complexity. Distribution costs, marketing expenses, sales commissions, and various other elements contribute to the intricate landscape of trade transaction costs.

Advanced Technologies for Complex Systems:

Addressing the complexities of the marketing chain necessitates more advanced technologies. Concepts like NFTs and metaverse technology emerge as potential solutions to streamline unnecessary movements of goods, reducing overall trade transaction costs.

In essence, gaining insights into logistics costs and trade transaction efficiency requires a holistic approach, considering trade-offs, embracing digitalization, and exploring cutting-edge technologies. The evolving landscape of global trade demands innovative solutions to enhance efficiency, reduce costs, and foster sustainable growth.

Topic 18: Green Logistics: Shaping a Sustainable Future

In the realm of logistics and international trade, where the movement of goods has witnessed unprecedented growth, the environmental impact has become a critical consideration. The carbon footprints left by sea transport, surface transportation, air transport, and operations at ports and airports raise concerns about the ecological implications. Addressing these challenges and aligning with global initiatives, the concept of "Green Logistics" emerges as a crucial paradigm shift.

Environmental Impact and Sustainability:

Balancing Economic Growth and Environmental Concerns:

The continuous expansion of international trade and logistics operations necessitates a delicate balance between economic growth and environmental sustainability. The increased movement of goods raises questions about the ecological impact on climate and the overall health of the planet.

Need for Green Logistics:

Recognizing the interconnectedness of the environment, global economy, and societal needs, there arises a pressing need for Green Logistics. This entails conducting logistics activities with the least possible ecological impact, aligning with the sustainability goals of both local governments and international bodies like the United Nations.

Call for Zero Ecological Impact:

Recent declarations on climate change emphasize the urgency of achieving zero ecological impact in logistics activities. The conventional approach of minimizing carbon footprints is evolving into a more ambitious goal of eliminating ecological harm entirely.

Redefining Global Business for Sustainability:

Digital Technologies for Environmental Minimization:

Initially, the focus was on incorporating digital technologies and advanced equipment into logistics systems to minimize the environmental impact. However, modern thinking goes beyond mere reduction and aims to redefine the entire concept of global business and international logistics.

Complete Digitization Through NFTs and Metaverses:

The avant-garde approach involves leveraging technologies like Non-Fungible Tokens (NFTs) and Metaverses for complete digitization. This transformative step envisions eliminating unnecessary movement of physical goods by trading virtual NFTs along the distribution chain. The goods would then be made available at the final layer of consumption.

System Perspective for Comprehensive Sustainability:

Green Logistics, in its modern interpretation, embraces a holistic system perspective. It transcends traditional boundaries and seeks to drastically reduce overall carbon footprints attributed to international trade and logistics activities. This forward-thinking approach acknowledges that time is of the essence in addressing environmental challenges.

Conclusion: A Sustainable Tomorrow:

In conclusion, the imperative for sustainable logistics practices has never been more pronounced. Green Logistics emerges as a beacon guiding the industry toward a future where economic prosperity coexists harmoniously with environmental preservation. By adopting innovative technologies, redefining global business practices, and embracing a comprehensive system perspective, the logistics sector can contribute significantly to building a sustainable tomorrow. The time to act is now, ensuring that future generations inherit a planet restored and preserved through conscientious logistics practices.

Topic 19: Chapter Takeaway: Navigating the Complexities of International Logistics

In this session, we delved into the dynamic landscape of international logistics and unearthed key takeaways that encapsulate the challenges and opportunities shaping the field. Let's distill the learnings:

High Growth of Trade:

The session illuminated the remarkable growth in global trade, providing consumers with unprecedented freedom, flexibility, and choices. The widespread welcome of this growth has transformed the logistics sector, leading to increased sea and air traffic and the burgeoning movement of goods.

Rising Complexity and Complications:

The surge in international logistics has brought about complexities and complications. The integration of artificial intelligence and digital technologies has automated numerous processes, making logistics operations more intricate. The sheer volume of cargo movement via various vehicles, be it sea, air, or train, has escalated.

Cost Optimization and Trade-Offs:

Amidst the growth, there's a paramount focus on optimizing logistics costs. This involves concerted efforts to reduce costs and find trade-offs among different cost components. The overarching aim is to enhance efficiency and make international trade economically viable.

Neglected Challenges and Concerns:

However, the single-minded pursuit of cost reduction has led to the neglect of other critical challenges and concerns. These challenges, as we explore in this session, extend beyond mere financial considerations.

Impact on Climate:

The expanded use of sea transport, in particular, has raised environmental concerns. The session underscores the vital role of seas in supporting marine life and absorbing carbon from the atmosphere. The impact of logistics activities on climate becomes a real and pressing concern, challenging the sustainability of current practices.

Climate Damage and Reversal:

Acknowledging the reality of climate change, the session prompts reflection on the role of international logistics in contributing to climate damage. Students and practitioners in logistics management are urged to adopt innovative solutions that serve as a win-win for humanity and the planet. The book's overarching objective aligns with this ethos: exploring ways to reverse climate damage within the realm of international logistics.

In conclusion, as we navigate the complexities of international logistics, it is imperative to strike a balance between economic objectives and environmental stewardship. The session takeaway emphasizes the need for sustainable practices, encouraging stakeholders to contribute positively to both human prosperity and the health of our planet.

Chapter 5: Different Modes of International Transportation

Topic 21: Chapter Overview

Greetings, everyone! I trust you're all set for an insightful exploration in today's session, where we delve into the pivotal subject of Modes of Transportation in International Logistics.

This topic lies at the core of effective supply chain management and international logistics, extending its influence across every facet of the global economy. Before we plunge into the intricacies of various transportation modes, let's pause to grasp the profound importance they hold in the realm of international logistics.

Picture the intricate web of global trade, where goods traverse the globe, connecting producers and consumers across continents. At the heart of this intricate network stand the modes of transportation, making this global dance of commodities possible. Consider the smartphone in your pocket, the clothes you wear, or the daily delights you savor – these items have likely journeyed vast distances, relying on different transportation modes.

The choice of transportation modes shapes the timeliness of your smartphone's arrival, the freshness of your clothes, and the quality of your food. In this session, spanning approximately 40 to 45 minutes, we'll navigate through the main modes of transportation in international logistics: road, rail, sea, air, and pipelines. Our exploration will encompass the characteristics, advantages, and limitations of each mode.

Moreover, we'll dive into practical scenarios, understanding when to opt for a specific mode over others. Whether you're a seasoned logistics professional honing your skills or a newcomer eager to learn, this session promises valuable insights.

By the session's end, you'll be armed with knowledge that can significantly impact your ability to make informed decisions on how goods traverse the global landscape. I invite each of you to actively engage in this session—ask questions, share experiences, and participate in discussions. Your contributions are immensely valuable as we collectively embark on this journey through the diverse world of transportation modes in international logistics.

Without further ado, let's commence this expedition into the fundamentals. As we progress, you'll gain a deeper understanding of the intricate logistics web that interconnects our world. Thank you for joining this session, and let's make it a collectively enriching experience for all involved.

Topic 22: Most Popular Modes of International Transportation

Greetings, and welcome to the foundational segment of our session, "Modes of Transportation in International Logistics." We are embarking on a journey to comprehend the essential transportation modes that serve as the lifelines of global goods movement.

In the intricate world of international logistics, understanding these modes is paramount to navigating the complexities effectively. So, what are these different modes that form the backbone of international trade? Let's begin our exploration.

1. Road Transportation: Roads act as the arteries of logistics, connecting local, regional, and international destinations. Trucks and vehicles emerge as the workhorses of road transportation, offering unmatched flexibility and accessibility. We'll delve into the nuances of road logistics, understanding its pivotal role in international trade.

2. Rail Transportation: Railways constitute the backbone of many countries' logistics networks, seamlessly crossing borders. Trains excel in efficiency, especially for long-distance overland transportation. In this segment, we'll uncover the intricacies of rail transportation and its integral part in international logistics.

3. Sea Transportation: Ships reign supreme over vast oceans and seas, facilitating a substantial portion of global trade. Containerization and the strategic role of ships in connecting continents will be on our radar. Let's explore how sea transportation shapes the international logistics landscape.

4. Air Transportation: For those prioritizing speed and reliability, air transportation emerges as the optimal choice. The aviation industry plays a crucial role in international logistics, particularly for high-value and time-sensitive cargoes. Our exploration will shed light on the significance of air transportation in the global logistics scenario.

5. Pipeline Transportation: Though not as visible as other modes, pipelines stand as unsung heroes for certain cargo types like oil and gas. We'll touch briefly on their significance in international logistics, understanding their unique contributions.

As we traverse through these transportation modes, remember a few key takeaways – each mode has distinct strengths and limitations. The choice of mode depends on factors such as cargo type, destination, time constraints, and cost efficiency. The strategic combination of these modes in intermodal and multimodal transportation often yields optimized logistics solutions.

By the end of this segment, you'll possess a solid foundation in understanding the role and significance of each transportation mode in international logistics. This knowledge will serve as a valuable compass as we progress through our session. So, let's dive into our first exploration: road transportation. Stay engaged, ask questions, and let's make the most of our time together in the dynamic world of transportation modes in international logistics.

Topic 23: Road Transportation in International Logistics

Let's hit the road, both figuratively and literally, as we dive into one of the most versatile and critical modes of transportation – road transportation. Roads serve as the lifeline of logistics, connecting cities, towns, and even remote areas. Today, our focus is on unraveling the characteristics, advantages, and limitations of road transportation in the realm of international logistics.

Characteristics of Road Transportation:

Flexibility: Unparalleled flexibility, allowing goods to reach locations with varying accessibility.

Last Mile Delivery: Excelling in the crucial last mile delivery, ensuring goods reach their final destinations, even in densely populated city centers.

Accessibility: Vast networks of roads providing access to regions where other modes of transportation may not be feasible.

Adaptability: Accommodating a wide range of cargo types, from perishable goods to oversized machinery.

Advantages of Road Transportation:

Speed and Timeliness: Often the fastest mode for short to medium distance shipments, ensuring timely deliveries.

Versatility: Well-suited for diverse cargo, from everyday consumer goods to construction materials.

Door-to-Door Services: Providing door-to-door services, simplifying logistics with direct pickup and delivery.

Reliability: Known for reliability, offering consistent schedules with minimal disruptions due to weather or natural obstacles.

Limitations of Road Transportation:

Distance Constraints: Less cost-effective and time-efficient for extremely long-distance hauls compared to rail or sea transportation.

Traffic Congestion: Possibilities of traffic congestions in urban areas causing delays and impacting delivery schedules.

Environmental Impact: Fuel consumption and emissions leading to sustainability challenges and environmental consequences.

Road Quality: Varying road quality affecting ease and speed of transportation.

Key Takeaways:

Road transportation is a cornerstone of international logistics, excelling in last-mile delivery and short to medium distance shipments. It offers speed, reliability, and door-to-door service but faces challenges with long distances, traffic, and environmental impact. Working in tandem with other modes like rail, sea, and air, road transportation ensures efficient and timely delivery of goods. In our next segment, we'll explore additional transportation modes and discover when to strategically employ each one for optimal results in the complex world of international logistics. Stay with me on this journey of knowledge and discovery.

Topic 24: Rail Transportation in International Logistics

Let's switch tracks and explore another vital mode of transportation in international logistics – Rail Transportation. Often referred to as the iron backbone of logistics, railways have played a crucial role in the movement of goods across countries and continents. In this segment, we will delve into the characteristics, advantages, and limitations of rail transportation.

Characteristics of Rail Transportation:

Efficiency: Highly efficient for transporting large volumes of cargo over long distances, particularly well-suited for hauling heavy and bulk goods.

Fixed Infrastructure: Railways have fixed infrastructure, offering predictable routes and schedules.

Connectivity: Rail networks connect various regions within a country and can extend across borders to facilitate international trade.

Safety: Trains are generally considered a safe mode of transportation, with lower accident rates compared to road transportation.

Advantages of Rail Transportation:

Cost-Effectiveness: More cost-effective than road or air transport, especially for long-distance hauls and heavy cargo.

Capacity: Substantial cargo capacity, making them ideal for transporting bulk goods such as coal, minerals, and grains.

Reliability: Consistent schedules, and fixed infrastructure reduce the impact of weather-related disruptions.

Environmental Benefits: Generally more fuel-efficient and produce fewer emissions per tonne of cargo compared to road transportation.

Limitations of Rail Transportation:

Infrastructural Constraints: Rail networks may not be as extensive in some regions, limiting accessibility.

Transshipment Needs: Cargo often requires transshipment between road and rail at specific points, introducing complexities.

Speed: Not as fast as air or road transportation, making them less suitable for time-sensitive shipments.

Cargo Type: Best suited for specific cargo types, such as bulk goods or heavy machinery, may not be suitable for perishable or high-value items.

Key Takeaways:

Rail transportation is highly efficient, cost-effective, and well-suited for long-distance transportation of bulk and heavy goods. It offers predictable schedules and has environmental advantages but may face infrastructural constraints and speed limitations. In the world of international logistics, rail transportation complements other modes like road, sea, and air, offering a valuable means of moving goods over land efficiently.

In our next segment, we will continue our journey exploring additional transportation modes and understanding when to strategically employ each one for optimal logistics outcomes. Stay on track with me.

Topic 25: Sea Transportation in International Logistics

Welcome to the segment where we set sail on the vast blue highways of international logistics. In this part of the session, we are delving into the world of sea transportation, a mode that plays a pivotal role in connecting continents and driving global trade. Join me as I explore the characteristics, advantages, and limitations of sea transportation.

Characteristics of Sea Transportation:

Scale: Ships have the capacity to transport massive quantities of cargo, making them ideal for bulk shipments and large-scale trade.

Global Reach: Sea routes connect major ports across the world, facilitating international trade on an unprecedented scale.

Containerization: The use of standardized containers has revolutionized sea transportation, streamlining cargo handling, enhancing efficiency, and minimizing costs.

Long Distances: Sea transport is particularly efficient for long-distance shipments, especially for goods traveling between different countries and continents.

Advantages of Sea Transportation:

Cost Effectiveness: On a per-tonne basis, sea transportation is often the most cost-effective mode, making it ideal for low-value, high-volume cargo.

Capacity: Ships can carry a wide range of cargo from raw materials to consumer goods, excelling at transporting goods in very large quantities.

Economies of Scale: The sheer size of container ships and bulk carriers allows for economies of scale that reduce per-unit transportation costs.

Environmental Efficiency: Ships are generally more fuel-efficient and produce fewer emissions per ton of cargo compared to other modes.

Limitations of Sea Transportation:

Speed: Ships are not the fastest mode of transportation, which can be a drawback for time-sensitive cargo.

Infrastructure: Ports and terminals must be equipped with accessibility, which can be a challenge in some regions, especially with mother ships.

Transshipment Requirement: Cargo often requires transshipment between sea and land-based transport, adding time and complexity.

Weather and Piracy Risks: Sea transportation can be vulnerable to weather-related delays, and in some regions, piracy risks.

Key Takeaways:

Sea transportation is a cost-effective, high-capacity mode suitable for long-distance transport of bulk and low-value goods. It offers global reach and environmental efficiency but may face speed and infrastructural challenges. In international logistics, sea transportation is an indispensable mode that connects countries and fuels a very large scale of global trade. It complements other modes like road, rail, and air, offering a vital means of transporting goods across countries and continents.

In our upcoming segments in this session, we'll continue our journey through transportation modes, gaining a deeper understanding of each one's role in the dynamic world of logistics. Stay with me as we sail ahead.

Topic 26: Air Transportation in International Logistics

Ladies and gentlemen, welcome to this part of the session where we take flight into the world of air transportation, a mode that offers unparalleled speed and efficiency in international logistics. In this part of our session, we will explore the characteristics, advantages, and limitations of air transportation.

Characteristics of Air Transportation:

Speed: Air transport is the fastest mode available, ensuring swift deliveries even across continents.

Global Reach: Airports dot the globe, allowing for seamless connectivity to almost any destination, and it can handle time-sensitive cargo.

Consistency: Air travel is known for its reliability, with consistent schedules and minimal weather-related disruptions.

Advantages of Air Transportation:

Speed and Timeliness: Air transport is unbeatable when it comes to ensuring time-sensitive deliveries, reducing lead times significantly.

Global Connectivity: Airports worldwide provide access to virtually any destination, even in remote or inaccessible areas.

Reliability: Air travel offers predictable schedules and high levels of cargo safety.

Safety and Security: Airports have stringent security measures in place, reducing the risk of theft and leakage.

Limitations of Air Transportation:

Cost: It is generally more expensive per ton-kilometer than any other mode, making it less suitable for low-value, high-volume cargo.

Low Capacity: Aircraft have limited cargo capacity compared to ships, which can be a constraint for very large shipments.

Environmental Impact: Air transportation has a higher carbon footprint per tonne of cargo compared to other modes.

Type of Cargo: While versatile, air transport may not be suitable for oversized or extremely heavy cargo.

Key Takeaways:

Air transportation is unmatched in terms of speed, making it ideal for time-sensitive and high-value cargo. It offers global reach and reliability but may face cost constraints and environmental considerations. In international logistics, air transportation is the mode of choice when speed and reliability are paramount. It complements other modes like road, rail, sea, and even pipeline transportation, offering a means to expedite goods across the globe.

In our upcoming segments, we will continue our journey through transportation modes, gaining deeper insights into their roles and applications in the intricate world of international logistics. Stay with me as we soar ahead.

Topic 27: Transportation by Pipelines in International Logistics

We venture into the world of pipeline transportation, a mode often hidden from plain sight but critical in ensuring the flow of vital resources in international logistics. In this segment of this session, we will explore the characteristics, advantages, and limitations of pipeline transportation.

Characteristics of Pipeline Transportation:

Specialization: Pipelines are specialized for transporting specific substances such as crude oil, natural gas, water, or minerals.

Point-to-Point: Pipeline networks are designed to transport resources from one fixed point to another, often over long distances.

Safety and Efficiency: Pipelines are known for their safety and efficiency, with minimal environmental impact when well maintained.

Constant Flow: Pipelines offer a continuous flow of resources, critical for industries like energy and petrochemicals.

Advantages of Pipeline Transportation:

Efficiency: Pipelines are incredibly efficient for transporting large quantities of resources, reducing transportation costs.

Environmental Impact: They have a relatively low environmental impact, with fewer emissions and reduced risk of spills compared to other modes.

Safety: Pipelines are equipped with safety measures, minimizing the risk of accidents and theft.

Continuous Flow: The constant flow of resources is essential for industries that rely on a steady supply, like energy and manufacturing.

Limitations of Pipeline Transportation:

Resource Specific: Pipelines are designed for specific resources, lacking versatility for transporting different types of cargo.

Infrastructure Investment: Building and maintaining pipeline networks require significant investment and infrastructure development.

Accessibility: Pipelines are not as accessible as other modes, primarily due to their point-to-point nature.

Regulatory Considerations: Pipelines are subject to regulatory oversight, impacting their operations and expansions.

Key Takeaways:

Pipeline transportation is highly efficient, cost-effective, and safe for specialized movement of liquids, gases, and some types of solids. It offers environmental benefits and constant resource flow but may face limitations related to resource specificity and infrastructure investments in international logistics. Pipeline transportation plays a critical role in ensuring the steady supply of resources, particularly in industries such as energy and petrochemical. While less visible than other modes, its significance cannot be understated.

In our upcoming segments, we will continue our journey through transportation modes, gaining deeper insights into their roles and applications in the dynamic world of international logistics. Stay with me as we explore further.

Topic 28: Summary of Advantages and Disadvantages of Each Transportation Mode

Here's a concise overview of the advantages and disadvantages of each transportation mode discussed:

Road Transportation:

Advantages:

Flexibility: Suitable for various destinations, including remote areas.

Last-mile delivery: Effective for delivering goods directly to final destinations.

Accessibility: Extensive road networks provide global access.

Adaptability: Accommodates a wide range of cargo types.

Disadvantages:

Distance constraints: Less cost-effective for extremely long-distance shipments.

Traffic congestion: Delays and disruptions in urban areas with heavy traffic.

Environmental impact: Contributes to pollution and carbon emissions.

Road quality: Conditions may vary, affecting efficiency.

Rail Transportation:

Advantages:

Efficiency: Efficient for transporting large volumes over long distances.

Predictability: Offers consistent schedules and routes.

Connectivity: Connects regions within a country and extends internationally.

Safety: Generally considered a safe mode of transportation.

Disadvantages:

Infrastructure constraints: Limited accessibility in certain regions.

Transshipment requirement: Cargo often requires transshipment between road and rail.

Speed: Slower compared to air transportation.

Cargo type: Best suited for bulk goods and heavy machinery.

Sea Transportation:

Advantages:

Cost-effectiveness: Efficient for long-distance and bulk shipments.

Large capacity: Transports massive quantities of cargo with economies of scale.

Global reach: Connects major ports worldwide.

Disadvantages:

Speed: Slower compared to air transportation.

Infrastructure: Ports must handle large vessels, including Motherships.

Transshipment requirement: Cargo often requires transshipment between sea and land transport.

Weather and piracy risks: Vulnerable to delays and piracy in certain regions.

Air Transportation:

Advantages:

Speed and timeliness: Ideal for time-sensitive and high-value cargo.

Global connectivity: Provides access to almost any destination.

Reliability: Consistent schedules and high cargo safety.

Security: Stringent security measures at airports worldwide.

Disadvantages:

High cost: Generally more expensive per ton-kilometer compared to other modes.

Less capacity: Limited cargo capacity compared to ships for large shipments.

Environmental impact: Higher carbon footprint per ton of cargo.

Cargo type: Versatile but not suitable for oversized or extremely heavy cargo.

Pipeline Transportation:

Advantages:

Efficiency: Highly efficient for specific resource transportation.

Environmental impact: Low emissions and minimal environmental impact.

Safety: Equipped with safety measures, ensuring a continuous flow.

Disadvantages:

Resource specific: Specialized for specific resources, lacks versatility.

Infrastructure investments: Requires substantial investments.

Accessibility: Not as accessible due to its point-to-point nature.

Regulatory considerations: Subject to oversight, impacting operations and expansion.

Each transportation mode has its unique strengths and limitations, making them suitable for different logistics scenarios based on cargo type, destination, time constraints, and cost efficiency. Effective logistics strategies often involve combining these modes strategically to optimize supply chain operations.

Topic 29: Choosing the Correct Mode of Transportation: A Strategic Approach

Having explored the diverse world of transportation modes, it's time to wear our logistics strategist hats and delve into the art of choosing the right mode. Selecting the most suitable mode is a pivotal decision in international logistics, impacting everything from cost to delivery terms.

Key Factors to Consider:

Cargo Type:

Consider the nature of your cargo – perishable goods, high-value electronics, bulky machinery, or bulk commodities. Each mode has cargo preferences.

Destination:

Evaluate the destination's accessibility and infrastructure for specific transportation modes. Proximity to ports, airports, railways, and roads matters.

Time Constraints:

Assess if your cargo is time-sensitive. Air transportation excels in speed, while sea or rail may be more time-effective for less urgent shipments.

Cost Efficiency:

Budget considerations are crucial. Calculate overall transportation costs, including freight charges, handling, storage, and potential delays. Balance cost against other factors.

Practical Examples:

Example 1: For shipping perishable fresh flowers from South America to Europe, air transportation is ideal for its unmatched speed.

Example 2: When moving heavy construction equipment from the Midwest to the Middle East, sea transportation followed by road or rail offers a balance of cost and time.

Example 3: Shipping high-value consumer electronics globally requires secure transportation, making air transportation the choice for speed and security.

Key Takeaways:

Cargo type, destination, time constraints, and cost efficiency are the cornerstones of mode selection.

A holistic approach and careful evaluation are essential to align the chosen mode with logistics goals.

The right choice of transportation mode can be a strategic advantage, driving success in global trade.

As you navigate the logistics decision maze, remember that it's not just about moving goods. It's about moving them efficiently, cost-effectively, and reliably. In the upcoming segments, we'll continue unraveling the intricacies of international logistics, exploring additional aspects contributing to successful supply chain management. Stay with me on this journey.

Topic 30: Discussion Questions:

Cargo Considerations:

How does the nature of the cargo influence the choice of transportation mode?

Can you provide examples of specific cargo types that are best suited for air, sea, road, rail, or pipeline transportation?

Destination and Infrastructure:

Why is it crucial to consider the destination's accessibility and infrastructure when selecting a transportation mode?

How might the proximity to ports, airports, railways, and roads impact the decision-making process?

Time Sensitivity:

In what scenarios would time sensitivity be a critical factor in choosing a transportation mode?

Can you think of industries or products where air transportation's speed is indispensable?

Cost Efficiency:

How would you balance cost considerations against other factors when deciding on a transportation mode?

What are some potential hidden costs in transportation that businesses should be mindful of?

Practical Examples:

Discuss the practical examples provided in the chapter. Can you think of additional examples that highlight the importance of cargo type, destination, time constraints, and cost efficiency?

Holistic Approach:

Why is a holistic approach essential in choosing the right transportation mode?

How might a decision that prioritizes only one factor, such as cost, impact overall logistics effectiveness?

Strategic Advantage:

In what ways can selecting the right transportation mode be a strategic advantage in global trade?

Can you share examples of businesses that have strategically utilized transportation modes to enhance their supply chain management?

Logistics Decision-Making:

What challenges might businesses face when making decisions about transportation modes in the dynamic field of international logistics?

How can continuous monitoring and adaptation contribute to more effective logistics decision-making?

Feel free to discuss these questions in a group setting, encouraging different perspectives and insights based on participants' experiences and knowledge of the logistics industry.

Topic 31: Chapter take away

Ladies and gentlemen, as we conclude our exploration of diverse transportation modes in international logistics, let's distill the key takeaways from this enlightening journey.

Firstly, diversity is the essence. Recognize that logistics demands tailored solutions. Each transportation mode has distinct characteristics, advantages, and limitations. There is no universal approach; it's about choosing what aligns with your specific needs.

A cargo-centric approach is paramount. Understand that the nature of your cargo shapes your mode selection. Whether it's perishables, machinery, or high-value electronics, cargo type is the starting point for informed decision-making.

Destinations matter significantly. Accessibility, infrastructure, and geographical location influence transportation mode choices. Consider these factors carefully to ensure an efficient and smooth logistics process.

Time sensitivity is key. For time-sensitive cargo, air transportation excels. However, for less urgent shipments, sea or rail may offer a more cost-effective solution. Balancing speed against cost is crucial.

Budget considerations are at the forefront. Analyze the overall cost of transportation, encompassing freight charges, handling, storage, and potential delays. Striking a balance between cost and other factors is essential.

Leverage technology's role. In the age of advanced logistics, technology provides real-time tracking, data analytics, and forecasting capabilities. Harness these tools to make informed decisions, especially in the international context.

Safety and security are non-negotiable. Prioritize cargo safety by choosing reputable carriers, considering cargo insurance, and utilizing technology for monitoring and enhancing security.

Explore multimodal opportunities. Combining transportation modes strategically provides flexibility and optimization. Uncover opportunities to leverage the strengths of different modes for complex logistics needs.

Navigate regulatory compliance. Be mindful of regional regulations as they can significantly impact mode selection. Stay informed and compliant to avoid delays and legal issues.

Adopt a holistic decision-making approach. Mode selection is an art that requires considering all factors collectively. Take a holistic view to make the best choices aligned with your logistics goals.

As we conclude this session, remember that logistics is more than moving goods; it's about doing so efficiently, cost-effectively, and reliably. The right choice of transportation mode can be a strategic advantage. Continue to stay curious, engaged, and explore the intricacies of this dynamic field.

Safe travels on your logistics journeys, and may your supply chain always run smoothly until our next section. Thank you all for your active participation and thoughtful questions. The world of logistics awaits with more insights and knowledge to gain.

Chapter 6: Inter Modal and Multi Modal Transportation

Topic 33: Chapter overview

Today, we are immersing ourselves in the realm of international logistics, with a particular focus on the pivotal concepts of intermodal and multimodal transportation.

In a nutshell, intermodal transportation acts as the Swiss Army knife of logistics. It involves the seamless movement of cargo utilizing various modes such as trucks, trains, ships, or airplanes. The uniqueness lies in the separation of each mode, with cargo transfers occurring between them at specific points. This approach offers versatility, enabling the optimization of different modes' strengths, leading to enhanced efficiency and cost-effectiveness.

Consider a scenario where goods journey from a Chicago factory to a retail store in Beijing, China. The cargo might transition from a truck to a rail terminal, then a train to a coastal port, and finally a container ship to reach China. Each leg of this journey utilizes a different mode, exemplifying intermodal transportation.

Now, let's shift our attention to multimodal transportation. Similar to intermodal, it involves multiple modes of transportation, but with a twist – all under a single transport operator or carrier. Unlike intermodal, where cargo may change hands between carriers, multimodal retains responsibility with one entity throughout the journey. This integrated approach simplifies management and tracking, especially beneficial for complex supply chains or time-sensitive cargo.

Imagine the same Chicago-to-Beijing shipment managed by a single logistics company overseeing the transfer between different modes. This integrated approach characterizes multimodal transportation.

The key difference lies in cargo management and responsibility. Intermodal involves handovers between carriers, while multimodal retains a single carrier's oversight throughout.

As you venture into the world of international logistics, understanding when to choose intermodal or multimodal transportation is crucial. Factors such as cargo type, destination, time constraints, and cost efficiency will influence your decision. Making the right choice can significantly impact the smoothness and efficiency of global supply chain operations.

In conclusion, intermodal and multimodal transportation are integral components of international logistics, each offering unique advantages suited to specific needs and circumstances. By grasping these concepts, you gain a valuable toolset to navigate the intricacies of global trade and shipping.

Thank you for your attention, and I trust you will find the upcoming chapters equally enlightening and informative.

Topic 34: Intermodal transportation

Let's dive into the intricacies of intermodal transportation, a crucial aspect of international logistics characterized by its distinctive feature of operating separate modes at different stages of the journey.

Versatility: Intermodal transportation is akin to having a toolkit with specialized tools. Each transport mode—trucks, trains, ships, and airplanes—brings unique strengths. Trucks excel in local deliveries, trains are efficient for long hauls, ships can carry vast quantities across oceans, and airplanes offer unparalleled speed. Strategically combining these modes optimizes efficiency and cost-effectiveness.

Integration and Coordination: Seamless integration and coordination of different transport modes are pivotal in intermodal transportation. Meticulous planning ensures smooth cargo transitions between modes at designated transfer points, minimizing delays and disruptions in the supply chain.

Flexibility: Intermodal transportation adapts to diverse cargo needs, accommodating a wide range of cargo types—from perishable goods to oversized equipment. The ability to select the most suitable mode for each leg of the journey adds valuable adaptability, particularly in international logistics.

Advantages:

Cost Efficiency: Intermodal transportation often leads to cost savings by utilizing the most cost-effective mode for each part of the journey. Combining rail and sea transport, for example, can be more economical than relying solely on trucks for long-distance journeys.

Reduced Environmental Impact: With a growing focus on environmental sustainability, intermodal transportation stands out as a greener option compared to relying solely on road transportation. Modes like trains and ships typically have lower emissions per unit of cargo moved.

Scalability and Capacity: Intermodal transportation can easily scale to meet growing demand. Additional transport modes can be incorporated without massive infrastructure investments, a crucial factor for businesses expanding their global reach.

Risk Mitigation: Diversifying transportation modes mitigates various risks. If one mode experiences a delay or issue, others can compensate, ensuring that goods reach their destination on time.

In summary, intermodal transportation is a logistics strategy that harnesses the strengths of various modes, offering versatility, cost efficiency, environmental benefits, scalability, and risk mitigation. It is a vital tool in international logistics, emphasizing efficiency, reliability, and cost-effectiveness.

Thank you for your attention to this crucial aspect of international logistics. In the next segment, we will delve into a comparison between intermodal and multimodal transportation, providing valuable insights for informed decision-making in your logistics endeavors. Stay tuned.

Topic 35: Examples of inter modal transportation scenarios

In this section of our book, "International Logistics Management and INCOTERMS 2020 Rules," we delve into the practical applications of intermodal transportation through various scenarios. These examples illustrate the seamless integration of different modes of transportation to facilitate efficient movement of goods.

Scenario 1: Transcontinental Journey Consider a manufacturer in Chicago needing to ship goods to a distributor in Shanghai. The journey begins with local trucking to a rail terminal, initiating a complex transcontinental route combining trucks, trains, and ships to bridge vast distances.

Scenario 2: Embracing Efficiency An agriculture producer in Kansas exports wheat to Europe. Utilizing rail transportation, the wheat travels to a coastal port where it's loaded onto a container ship, optimizing efficiency for the landlocked state.

Scenario 3: Crossing Oceans with Ease A clothing manufacturer in Bangladesh exports garments to North America. Trucks transport goods to a seaport, where they embark on a container ship journey. Upon arrival, trucks handle the final leg, ensuring timely delivery to retail stores.

Scenario 4: Combining Air and Ground Transport An electronics manufacturer in South Korea ships high-value products to the US. Starting with a truck ride to the airport, goods are swiftly loaded onto an international flight. Upon arrival, trucks ensure the final mile delivery to the customer.

Scenario 5: Seasonal Agricultural Exports A fruit grower in Chile exports fresh produce worldwide. Trucks transport goods to a refrigerated rail terminal, ensuring freshness during transit to a seaport. Container ships then distribute the produce globally.

These scenarios exemplify the strategic utilization of intermodal transportation, optimizing each leg of the journey for cost-effectiveness, efficiency, and timely delivery. Intermodal transportation offers versatility and adaptability, tailoring logistics solutions to specific needs, ultimately distinguishing successful logistics professionals. In our exploration of international logistics, understanding these concepts and their real-world applications is paramount. In the next part of our session, we will delve into multimodal transportation, providing a comprehensive understanding of its distinctions and suitability for various logistics needs. Thank you for your attention.

Topic 36: Multimodal Transportation

In this segment of our International Logistics Management book, we'll shift our focus to another essential aspect of logistics: multimodal transportation. Over the next few minutes, we'll define this concept and explore its distinct characteristics and notable advantages.

First things first, what is multimodal transportation? It's a logistics strategy akin to intermodal transportation, involving the integration of multiple modes of transportation under a single operator or carrier. Unlike intermodal, where cargo may change hands between different carriers, multimodal transportation ensures that one entity manages the entire journey from origin to destination.

Now, let's delve into the key characteristics that set multimodal transportation apart.

Seamless Integration: Multimodal transportation seamlessly integrates various modes such as trucks, trains, ships, or airplanes. This coordination ensures smooth transitions between modes under the oversight of a single entity.

Single Carrier Responsibility: With multimodal transportation, cargo remains under the care of one carrier throughout its journey. This simplifies logistics management for customers, offering a unified approach and reducing complexities.

Streamlined Tracking and Accountability: Having one entity oversee the entire transportation chain simplifies tracking and ensures accountability. From origin to destination, the carrier is responsible for safe and timely delivery, enhancing supply chain visibility and customer satisfaction.

Flexibility and Efficiency: Multimodal transportation adapts to diverse cargo requirements, whether shipping perishables, oversize equipment, or standard products. This flexibility contributes to overall logistics efficiency.

Now, let's explore the advantages of multimodal transportation.

Simplified Logistics Management: With one carrier overseeing the journey, logistics professionals can efficiently coordinate complex shipments, benefiting companies with intricate supply chains.

Enhanced Accountability: Multimodal transportation enhances accountability, with a single carrier responsible for cargo safety and timely delivery, minimizing risks of miscommunication and transfer issues.

Improved Cargo Security: By reducing handovers and transfers, multimodal transportation enhances cargo security, minimizing opportunities for theft, damage, or loss.

Time and Cost Efficiency: Ultimately, multimodal transportation aims for time and cost efficiency by optimizing transportation modes and routes, reducing overall costs while ensuring timely delivery.

In conclusion, multimodal transportation prioritizes seamless integration and accountability, offering simplified logistics management, enhanced cargo security, and potential cost and time savings. Understanding these concepts is crucial in navigating the complex landscape of international logistics.

Thank you for your attention. In the next part of our session, we'll explore specific examples and scenarios where multimodal transportation shines, demonstrating its practical applications in international logistics.

Topic 37: Examples of multi modal transportation scenarios

In this part of our International Logistics Management book, we'll explore multimodal transportation through real-world examples, showcasing the versatility of this logistics strategy.

Let's dive into some practical scenarios:

Scenario 1: Cross-Continental Track Imagine a manufacturer in Los Angeles needing to transport machinery to a construction site in New York. Using a multimodal approach, the cargo starts with truck transportation to a nearby rail terminal. Specialized rail cars then carry the machinery across the country to a rail yard closer to the site, where trucks complete the journey to the construction site.

Scenario 2: Temperature-Sensitive Pharmaceuticals A pharmaceutical company in Europe ships temperature-sensitive vaccines to a distribution center in Africa. The cargo travels by truck to an international airport, where it's loaded onto a refrigerated cargo plane. Upon arrival in Africa, the vaccines are seamlessly transferred to refrigerated trucks, ensuring proper temperature control throughout the journey.

Scenario 3: International Auto Exports An automaker in Japan exports cars to dealerships in Australia. Trucks transport the vehicles to a nearby seaport, where they're loaded onto roll-on/roll-off vessels designed for efficient loading and unloading. Upon arrival in Australia, trucks distribute the cars to dealerships across the country.

In these scenarios, we witness the efficiency of multimodal transportation, tailored to the specific needs of each cargo. By integrating various transportation modes, including trucks, trains, ships, and airplanes, we overcome geographical challenges, manage temperature-sensitive cargo, and efficiently transport vehicles to international markets.

Multimodal transportation empowers logistics professionals to customize solutions for diverse cargo types and destinations, optimizing efficiency and effectiveness.

Thank you for your attention to these practical examples of multimodal transportation. In our next segment, we'll compare intermodal and multimodal transportation, aiding you in making informed decisions for your logistics endeavors.

Topic 38: Key differences between intermodal and multimodal transportation

In this part of our book, we'll delineate the key differences between intermodal and multimodal transportation. Understanding these disparities will equip you to navigate the dynamic world of international logistics more effectively.

Let's dive into the crucial distinctions:

Ownership and Responsibility of Cargo: In intermodal transportation, cargo may change hands between different carriers as it switches modes. This distributed responsibility among multiple entities can complicate accountability and coordination. Conversely, in multimodal transportation, cargo remains under the care of one carrier throughout its journey, simplifying logistics management and providing a unified point of accountability.

Simplicity and Complexity: Intermodal transportation often involves multiple carriers and transfer points, adding layers of complexity to the logistics chain. Each transition between modes requires careful coordination and may introduce opportunities for miscommunication or delays. In contrast, multimodal transportation streamlines the process by having a single carrier oversee the entire journey, reducing complexities associated with multiple handovers.

Flexibility and Cost Considerations: Intermodal transportation offers high flexibility in selecting the most suitable mode of transport for each leg of the journey, advantageous for diverse cargo types and complex supply chains. However, it can incur added costs and coordination efforts due to involvement of multiple carriers. Multimodal transportation, while still flexible, simplifies decision-making by having one carrier manage the entire journey. This holistic approach allows for more efficient cost management as the carrier optimizes transportation modes and routes, balancing flexibility and cost-effectiveness.

In summary, the main differences between intermodal and multimodal transportation revolve around the ownership and responsibility of cargo, the simplicity or complexity of the logistics process, and the balance between flexibility and cost considerations. As you navigate the logistics landscape, understanding these distinctions will be pivotal in selecting the most suitable approach for your specific cargo and supply chain needs.

Thank you for your attention to these critical differences. In the next part of our book, we'll explore when to choose intermodal or multimodal transportation, providing practical insights for your logistics decision-making.

Topic 39: When to Choose Intermodal or Multimodal?

Before we wrap up our discussion, let's explore the considerations for deciding between intermodal and multimodal transportation. This decision is crucial in optimizing logistics operations and meeting business objectives.

Cargo Type: Consider the nature of your goods. Are they perishable, fragile, oversized, or standard consumer products? Intermodal transportation's flexibility may suit various cargo types with specific handling requirements, while multimodal transportation may be preferable for goods with less specialized handling needs.

Destination: The destination of your cargo is vital. Are you shipping domestically or internationally? Consider if you need to reach a remote area or a major urban center. Multimodal transportation, with its single carrier oversight, may be favored for straightforward routes or when delivering to major urban hubs.

Time Constraints: Time sensitivity is paramount in logistics. Determine if your shipments need to reach their destination quickly or if there's flexibility in the delivery schedule. For urgent shipments, multimodal transportation's streamlined coordination may reduce risks of delays, while intermodal transportation can still be effective with meticulous planning.

Cost Efficiency: Optimizing costs while maintaining service quality is essential. Intermodal transportation can provide cost efficiency by selecting the most cost-effective mode for each leg of the journey.

Multimodal transportation offers potential cost savings through holistic management of transportation modes. Conduct careful cost analysis to make informed choices.

It's important to balance these considerations as they often intersect. For example, a time-sensitive, fragile cargo bound for a remote destination may find the most efficient and reliable solution through multimodal transportation, despite potential higher costs.

In conclusion, choosing between intermodal and multimodal transportation depends on several factors. By evaluating cargo nature, destination, time constraints, and cost efficiency, you can optimize logistics operations. Remember, the right choice varies from one shipment to another, and a deep understanding of these factors guides informed logistics decisions aligned with business objectives.

Thank you for your attention to these critical considerations. In our next and final segment, we'll discuss key takeaways from this session.

Topic 40: Chapter takeaway

As we conclude this session of our International Logistics Management book, let's recap the key takeaways and underscore the critical importance of making informed decisions about transportation modes in international logistics management.

Throughout our session, we've delved into a wealth of valuable insights:

We began by defining and differentiating between intermodal and multimodal transportation, highlighting their influence on the flow of goods and responsibility of the cargo.

We explored real-life examples of both intermodal and multimodal transportation scenarios, showcasing their versatility and efficiency in diverse logistics contexts.

Next, we examined the main differences between these approaches, including cargo ownership, logistics complexity, and flexibility and cost considerations.

We discussed the factors influencing the decision to choose between intermodal and multimodal transportation, emphasizing the pivotal role of cargo type, destination, time constraints, and cost efficiency.

We underscored the importance of making informed decisions in international logistics, as efficiency and customer satisfaction are paramount. Informed decisions can lead to streamlined operations, reduced costs, timely deliveries, and ultimately, enhanced customer satisfaction.

We learned that informed decision-making can provide a competitive advantage, improve market responsiveness, and contribute to sustainability goals by reducing emissions and minimizing waste.

In conclusion, international logistics is dynamic and complex. By understanding transportation modes' nuances and making informed decisions, you position your business for success in the global marketplace. Your ability to adapt, optimize, and choose the right logistics strategy will be crucial in achieving your business objectives.

Thank you for your active participation throughout this session. As we navigate the future of international logistics and supply chain management, remember that knowledge and informed decision-making will be your most valuable assets. Safe journeys, and may your logistics endeavors be as efficient as they are rewarding.

Chapter 7: The Role of Intermediaries

Topic 41: Chapter Overview

Friends, welcome back to this new chapter of our book, International Logistics Management. In this session, we will delve into understanding the different types of logistics service providers and their roles within the logistics ecosystem.

There are various ways to classify logistics service providers, and in this session, we'll focus on the nature of these providers based on the number of parties involved. We'll explore terms like 1PL, 2PL, 3PL, 4PL, and even 5PL logistics service providers, shedding light on their distinct roles and positions in logistics management.

Our discussion will cover the following key points:

Understanding the roles and differences between 1PL, 2PL, 3PL, 4PL, and 5PL service providers.

Exploring common concepts and terms associated with each type of service provider, such as asset-based and non-asset-based providers.

Discussing related concepts like reverse logistics, aggregators, and consolidators to deepen our understanding of the logistics landscape.

We'll start by defining what each type of logistics service provider entails, beginning with 1PL logistics service providers. Stay tuned as we unravel the complexities and nuances of the logistics industry, gaining valuable insights into the roles and functions of intermediaries in logistics management.

Let's embark on this journey to explore the diverse world of logistics service providers and their vital contributions to the global supply chain.

Topic 42: Common classification of logistics services providers and what are their roles?

In understanding the landscape of logistics service providers, we encounter various classifications that delineate their roles and functions within the supply chain. Let's explore these common classifications and elucidate their respective roles:

First Party Logistics (1PL):

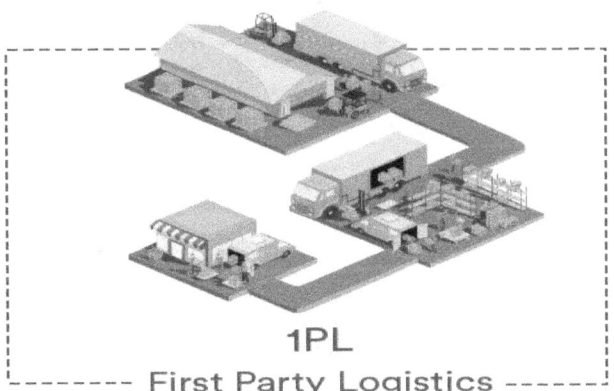

In 1PL logistics, the provider, often a firm or individual, possesses its own cargo and assets, such as warehouses or vehicles. They distribute their goods using these assets, ensuring direct control over the transportation process. Examples include small vendors managing their own B2B distribution networks.

Second Party Logistics (2PL):

2PL providers engage in moving goods using either their own fleet of vehicles or contracted carriers. Unlike 1PL, 2PL may transport goods for other parties, such as wholesale distributors or companies specializing in specific cargo movements like coal or cement transportation.

Third Party Logistics (3PL):

Also known as 3PL, these providers not only transport goods but also offer additional logistics services like warehousing, terminal handling, and customs brokerage. They act as intermediaries facilitating various aspects of logistics operations, including storage, handling, and clearance, both domestically and internationally.

Fourth Party Logistics (4PL):

4PL providers serve as overseers of multiple 3PL entities. They coordinate and integrate the services of various third-party logistics providers, each specializing in different areas of logistics, to streamline supply chain operations. Examples include supply chain consultants and lead logistics providers offering comprehensive logistics solutions.

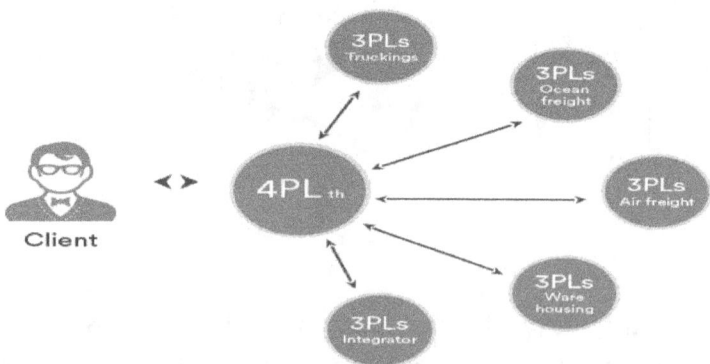

Fifth Party Logistics (5PL):

5PL providers function as logistics aggregators, consolidating demand from multiple 3PL entities to negotiate favorable rates with main carriers such as shipping lines, airlines, or trucking companies. By aggregating demand in bulk volumes, they aim to secure cost-effective transportation solutions for their clients.

Each classification offers distinct advantages and serves specific roles within the logistics ecosystem, depending on their assets, expertise, and specialization. Understanding these classifications enables businesses to choose the most suitable logistics service provider that aligns with their unique supply chain requirements and objectives.

Topic 43: Aggregators and Consolidators

To comprehend the significance of aggregators and consolidators in logistics, it's essential to grasp their roles in optimizing cargo movements and securing favorable rates. Let's delve into the concept:

Aggregators and Consolidators: In logistics, aggregators and consolidators play pivotal roles in optimizing cargo movements and leveraging economies of scale to negotiate advantageous rates with carriers. These entities facilitate the consolidation and aggregation of cargo or demand from multiple clients, thereby enhancing efficiency and cost-effectiveness in transportation.

Aggregation of Cargo: Aggregation pertains to the process of consolidating individual shipments or cargo from various clients into larger, more economically viable units. This consolidation allows for the optimization of space utilization within transportation containers, such as standard shipping containers used in international trade. By combining multiple smaller shipments into larger loads, aggregators can achieve economies of scale and negotiate better rates with carriers.

Aggregation of Demand: In addition to aggregating cargo, aggregators also consolidate demand from multiple clients to enhance bargaining power with carriers. For instance, fifth-party logistics providers may aggregate demand for shipping services across different clients, pooling their requirements to secure more favorable pricing and terms from main carriers. By consolidating demand, these providers can negotiate volume discounts and achieve cost savings for their clients.

Role in Containerization: The advent of containerization has revolutionized cargo transportation by standardizing container sizes and streamlining handling processes. Aggregators and consolidators play a crucial role in optimizing container utilization by filling containers to capacity, whether through full container load (FCL) or less than container load (LCL) shipments. They ensure efficient stuffing of containers while catering to varying shipment sizes and demand volumes.

Conclusion: In summary, aggregators and consolidators serve as key intermediaries in logistics, facilitating the efficient consolidation of cargo and demand to achieve economies of scale and cost savings. By optimizing cargo movements and leveraging aggregated volumes, these entities contribute to enhanced efficiency, cost-effectiveness, and competitiveness in the global supply chain. Understanding their roles is essential for businesses seeking to optimize their logistics operations and secure favorable transportation solutions.

Topic 44: Inbound and outbound logistics types

Understanding inbound and outbound logistics is crucial for any business to effectively manage its supply chain operations. Let's break down these concepts:

Inbound Logistics: Inbound logistics refers to the management of materials, components, or goods that flow into a company's premises. The nature of inbound logistics varies depending on the core business activities of the company:

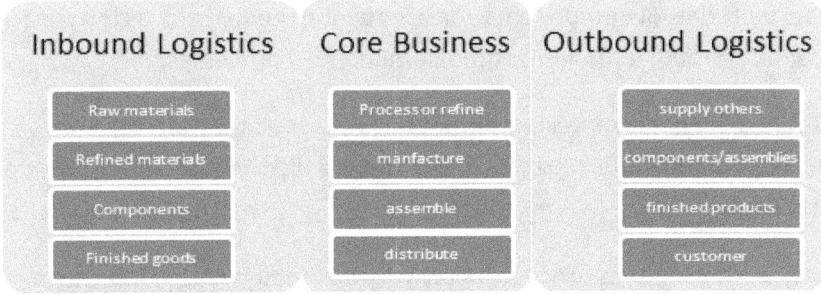

For manufacturing or refining companies, inbound logistics typically involves the procurement of raw materials needed for production. Raw materials are sourced from suppliers and transported to the manufacturing facility.

For manufacturers, inbound logistics may involve receiving components and assemblies from suppliers that are used in the production process.

Companies engaged in assembling work receive components as part of their inbound logistics process.

Outbound Logistics: Outbound logistics, on the other hand, involves the movement of finished products from the company's premises to its customers or distribution channels. Again, the nature of outbound logistics depends on the core business activities:

For manufacturing companies, outbound logistics include the distribution of finished products to wholesalers, retailers, or end consumers.

Distributors manage outbound logistics by delivering finished goods from warehouses to customers or retail outlets.

E-commerce companies handle outbound logistics by shipping orders directly to customers after processing.

Core Business and Logistics: The distinction between inbound and outbound logistics is closely tied to a company's core business activities:

Raw materials or components constitute inbound logistics as they are essential inputs for manufacturing or assembly processes.

Finished products represent outbound logistics as they are the end result of manufacturing or assembly and are distributed to customers or end users.

The specific logistics processes may vary depending on the industry and business model, but the fundamental principles remain the same.

Conclusion: In summary, inbound and outbound logistics are integral components of a company's supply chain management. By efficiently managing the flow of materials and products into and out of the organization, businesses can optimize their operations, reduce costs, and enhance customer satisfaction. Understanding the dynamics of inbound and outbound logistics is essential for businesses to streamline their supply chain processes and remain competitive in today's market.

Topic 45: Cold Chain Logistics

Cold chain logistics, also known as chill chain logistics, is a specialized type of logistics designed to transport temperature-sensitive goods safely and efficiently. This concept is vital for products that require controlled temperatures to maintain their quality and integrity throughout the supply chain journey. Let's delve into the key aspects of cold chain logistics:

Nature of Cold Chain Goods: Cold chain logistics primarily caters to goods that are sensitive to temperature variations. These include:

Perishable food items like fresh fruits, vegetables, and processed foods.

Beverages that can degrade or spoil if exposed to unfavorable temperatures.

Biopharmaceutical products, including vaccines and other medical solutions, which require precise temperature control to maintain their efficacy.

Importance of Temperature Control: The critical aspect of cold chain logistics is maintaining consistent temperature conditions throughout the transportation process. Any deviation from the required temperature range can compromise the quality and safety of the goods, leading to spoilage or degradation. Therefore, specialized equipment, such as refrigerated trucks, cold storage facilities, and temperature monitoring systems, are employed to ensure precise temperature control at every stage of the logistics chain.

Examples of Cold Chain Logistics:

Transportation of perishable goods from farms to retail outlets, ensuring that fresh produce remains crisp and nutritious.

Distribution of vaccines and pharmaceutical products to healthcare facilities, safeguarding their potency and effectiveness.

Delivery of temperature-sensitive food items to restaurants and supermarkets, preserving their freshness and taste.

Key Considerations:

Temperature Monitoring: Continuous monitoring of temperature conditions is crucial to identify and address any deviations promptly.

Packaging: Insulated packaging and temperature-controlled containers help maintain the desired temperature levels during transit.

Regulatory Compliance: Compliance with regulations and standards governing cold chain logistics, such as Good Distribution Practice (GDP) guidelines, is essential to ensure product safety and regulatory compliance.

Conclusion: In conclusion, cold chain logistics plays a vital role in ensuring the integrity and safety of temperature-sensitive goods throughout the supply chain. By employing specialized equipment, rigorous temperature monitoring, and adherence to regulatory standards, companies can effectively manage cold chain logistics and deliver high-quality products to consumers. Understanding the principles of cold chain logistics is essential for businesses operating in industries where temperature control is critical to product quality and customer satisfaction.

Topic 46: Reverse logistics

Reverse logistics refers to the processes involved in managing the return, recycling, or disposal of products after they have been delivered to the end consumer. Let's explore the key aspects of reverse logistics:

Reverse Logistics Supply Chain

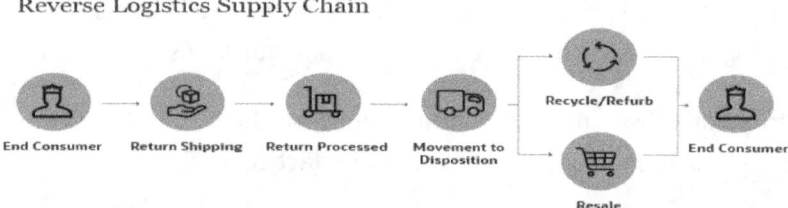

Role of Logistic Providers: After a customer receives a product, scenarios such as product returns or recycling may necessitate the involvement of logistic providers in the form of reverse logistics. Even if the end consumer is responsible for product disposal, logistic providers may play a role in facilitating the process.

Reverse Logistics Supply Chain: The reverse logistics supply chain typically involves the following steps:

Return Shipping: Products are shipped back to the seller or designated return center.

Movement to Disposition: Reverse logistics providers transport the returned goods to determine their fate.

Disposition Processing: Depending on the condition of the returned products, they may undergo recycling, refurbishing, or resale processes. These products may then be reintroduced into the market for resale or distribution to other end consumers.

Types of Reverse Logistics Providers: Reverse logistics service providers specialize in managing the reverse flow of goods and may offer services such as recycling, refurbishing, or resale. These providers play a crucial role in efficiently handling returned products and minimizing waste in the supply chain.

Importance of Understanding Reverse Logistics: Understanding the concept of reverse logistics is essential for comprehensively managing the logistics process. By grasping the roles and functions of reverse logistics providers, businesses can effectively address product returns, minimize waste, and optimize resource utilization in the supply chain.

Conclusion: In conclusion, reverse logistics is a vital component of the logistics process, involving the management of returned products and their disposition. By incorporating reverse logistics strategies, businesses can efficiently handle product returns, minimize waste, and enhance sustainability in the supply chain. Understanding the principles of reverse logistics is crucial for optimizing logistics operations and ensuring customer

Topic 47: Assets and Non Assets Based LSPs

Assets and non-assets-based logistics service providers (LSPs) play distinct roles in the logistics industry. Let's delve into the differences between these two types:

Assets-Based LSPs: Assets-based LSPs, including first-party logistics (1PL), second-party logistics (2PL), and third-party logistics (3PL) providers, possess tangible resources such as warehouses, carriers, and handling equipment. These resources enable them to directly manage and execute various logistics functions, from storage to transportation. Assets-based LSPs rely on their physical infrastructure to deliver services efficiently and effectively.

Non-Assets-Based LSPs: In contrast, non-assets-based LSPs, such as fourth-party logistics (4PL) and fifth-party logistics (5PL) providers, operate without owning significant physical assets. Instead, they leverage their expertise in logistics management, innovation, and integration to optimize supply chain processes. Non-assets-based LSPs focus on orchestrating and coordinating logistics activities across multiple parties, aiming to streamline operations, reduce costs, and enhance overall efficiency.

Differentiating Factors: The key distinction between assets-based and non-assets-based LSPs lies in their reliance on physical infrastructure versus management expertise and integration capabilities. While assets-based LSPs offer direct control over logistics operations, non-assets-based LSPs excel in strategic planning, coordination, and optimization of supply chain activities.

Specialization: Furthermore, LSPs may specialize in specific services or industries, such as cold chain logistics or reverse logistics. Specialized LSPs address unique requirements, such as transporting temperature-sensitive goods or managing product returns, catering to clients with specialized needs and ensuring the efficient handling of specialized cargo.

Conclusion: Understanding the roles and classifications of logistics service providers, whether assets-based or non-assets-based, is crucial for optimizing supply chain management. By recognizing the strengths and capabilities of different types of LSPs, businesses can make informed decisions when selecting logistics partners and effectively meet their logistics requirements. Whether it's leveraging tangible assets or expertise in logistics management, each type of LSP contributes uniquely to the efficient functioning of the logistics ecosystem.

Chapter Conclusion

As we conclude this chapter on understanding logistics service providers, let's recap the key takeaways:

Diverse Roles: We explored the various classifications of logistics service providers, ranging from assets-based (1PL, 2PL, 3PL) to non-assets-based (4PL, 5PL). Each type plays a distinct role in the logistics ecosystem, either through tangible resources or management expertise.

Specialization: LSPs may specialize in specific services or industries, such as cold chain logistics or reverse logistics. Specialized providers cater to unique requirements, ensuring efficient handling of specialized cargo and meeting clients' specific needs.

Efficiency and Optimization: Whether assets-based or non-assets-based, LSPs contribute to optimizing supply chain processes. Assets-based providers offer direct control over logistics operations, while non-assets-based providers excel in strategic planning and coordination.

Client-Centric Approach: Understanding the strengths and capabilities of different LSPs is essential for businesses to make informed decisions when selecting logistics partners. By aligning with the right provider, businesses can enhance efficiency, reduce costs, and meet their logistics requirements effectively.

In conclusion, logistics service providers play a crucial role in the smooth functioning of supply chains. By leveraging their expertise and resources, businesses can navigate the complexities of logistics operations and achieve operational excellence. As businesses continue to evolve, understanding the nuances of logistics service providers will remain instrumental in optimizing supply chain management and driving success in the global marketplace.

Chapter 8: Unitization, Palletization and Standardization

Topic 48: Chapter Overview

Welcome, everyone, to the next chapter in our International Logistics Management book. In this session, we'll delve into the transformative role of unitization and standardization in revolutionizing cargo movement within the realm of international logistics.

Over the years, innovative ideas such as unitization, palletization, and optimized cargo stowing have reshaped the landscape of logistics management. These concepts, driven by scientific ingenuity and mechanized processes, have not only increased the speed and safety of cargo movement but also made it more cost-effective and efficient.

Our agenda for this session is to explore the fundamentals of unitization and understand its significance in cargo handling. We'll delve into the evolution of pallets and the importance of standardization in cargo handling, focusing on the standardized sizes of pallets and their implications.

Furthermore, we'll examine various methods of palletization and their respective impacts on cargo handling processes. By understanding the intricacies of palletization, you'll gain insights into its role and significance in modern logistics practices.

Lastly, we'll discuss the critical aspect of cargo stowing on ships, considering the increased size of vessels necessitated by unitization and palletization. We'll explore the strategic planning involved in cargo placement and the tangible benefits of adopting palletization in international logistics management.

Through this session, we aim to provide you with a comprehensive understanding of unitization, palletization, and cargo stowing, and their transformative impact on international logistics. Join us as we unravel the real benefits of these innovative ideas and their role in shaping the future of logistics management.

Topic 49: Unitization

Unitization is a fundamental concept in the realm of international logistics management, especially when dealing with large shipments, particularly in sea freight. As the volume of cargo increases, individual boxes or cartons become impractical for handling. Instead, the concept of unitization involves grouping these smaller packages into standardized units, typically pallets.

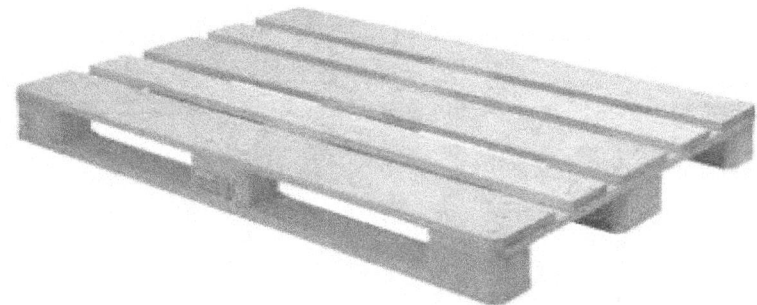

Pallets serve as the building blocks of unitization, allowing for the efficient handling of cargo using mechanized equipment such as forklifts and cranes. By clustering smaller packages into pallets, the handling process becomes streamlined, minimizing damages, reducing handling time, and improving overall productivity in the transport delivery chain.

Moreover, unitization extends beyond pallets to standardized containers, such as the common 40ft containers used in modern shipping. These containers provide a further level of unitization, allowing for the consolidation of pallets into larger packages that can be seamlessly handled by cargo vessels, trucks, and other transportation vehicles.

The standardization of pallet and container sizes further enhances efficiency, ensuring compatibility with mechanized handling equipment and facilitating rapid turnaround times. Ultimately, unitization optimizes cargo handling processes, increases efficiency, and contributes to the smooth and cost-effective movement of goods in international logistics management.

Unitization, driven by the concept of grouping smaller packages into larger, standardized units, has revolutionized the logistics landscape by enhancing efficiency, reducing costs, and improving overall supply chain performance. This fundamental principle finds extensive application in various sectors of international trade, particularly in sea freight where handling large volumes of cargo is routine.

At its core, unitization simplifies the handling process by aggregating smaller packages into standardized units like pallets. These pallets serve as the basic building blocks of cargo consolidation, enabling swift and systematic loading and unloading procedures. By clustering individual cartons or boxes into pallets, the need for labor-intensive manual handling is minimized, while the risk of damages and losses during transit is significantly reduced.

Furthermore, the standardization of pallet sizes ensures compatibility with mechanized handling equipment such as forklifts and conveyor systems. This compatibility streamlines operations at ports, warehouses, and distribution centers, allowing for seamless movement of palletized cargo throughout the supply chain. As a result, the turnaround time for loading and unloading cargo is expedited, optimizing the utilization of transportation assets and resources.

In addition to pallets, unitization extends to standardized containers, which represent the next level of cargo consolidation. Containers, such as the widely used 40ft steel containers, offer a robust and uniform means of transporting palletized goods across vast distances. By accommodating multiple pallets within a single container, space utilization is maximized, leading to cost savings and improved transportation efficiency.

The benefits of unitization are manifold and extend beyond operational enhancements to encompass broader economic and environmental advantages. By minimizing handling time and maximizing cargo capacity, unitization contributes to lower transportation costs, reduced fuel consumption, and fewer emissions per unit of cargo transported. Moreover, the standardized nature of unitized cargo simplifies inventory management, enhances supply chain visibility, and promotes interoperability across global trade networks.

In conclusion, unitization stands as a cornerstone of modern logistics practices, offering a systematic approach to cargo handling and transportation. Through the consolidation of smaller packages into standardized units, unitization optimizes supply chain operations, fosters efficiency gains, and drives sustainable growth in international trade. As global trade continues to evolve, the principles of unitization will remain essential for meeting the demands of an interconnected and dynamic marketplace.

Topic 50: Palletization

Palletization is a pivotal aspect of modern logistics, facilitating the efficient handling, storage, and transportation of goods. At its core, palletization involves the use of specialized bases, known as pallets, to consolidate and unitize cargo for streamlined operations. These pallets come in various types, including standard pallets, slip sheet pallets, and skid pallets, each tailored to specific handling requirements and equipment capabilities.

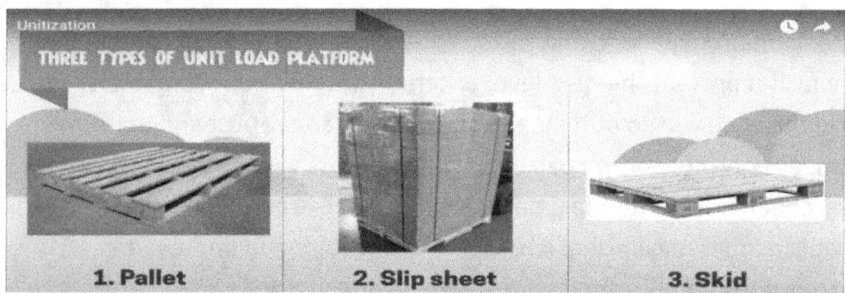

Standard pallets, slip sheet pallets, and skid pallets serve as the foundation for palletization, providing a stable platform for stacking and securing cargo. The choice of pallet type depends on factors such as product characteristics, handling methods, and storage constraints. While standard pallets are widely used for their versatility and compatibility with forklifts and conveyors, slip sheet pallets offer a space-saving alternative, ideal for automated handling systems. Skid pallets, on the other hand, provide a simple yet effective solution for heavy or irregularly shaped loads.

Palletization processes can vary from manual and semi-automatic to fully automated and even robotic, depending on the scale of operations and technological capabilities. Manual palletization involves hand-stacking cargo onto pallets, while automated systems utilize machinery and robotics for precise and efficient handling. These systems enhance productivity, reduce labor costs, and minimize the risk of errors associated with manual handling.

In addition to pallet types and handling methods, pallets themselves can be designed for specific functions and environments. Stackable pallets allow for efficient storage and transportation by enabling vertical stacking, while two-way or four-way entry designs accommodate different forklift configurations. Furthermore, pallets may be shrink-wrapped, stretch-wrapped, or strapped for added stability and security during transit.

Material-wise, pallets can be constructed from various materials, including wood, plastic, or metal, with each offering unique benefits in terms of durability, weight-bearing capacity, and recyclability. While permanent pallets provide long-term reliability, disposable pallets offer convenience and cost-effectiveness, particularly for one-time or short-term use scenarios.

Overall, palletization plays a crucial role in optimizing supply chain operations, facilitating the seamless movement of goods from production facilities to distribution centers and ultimately to end-users. By standardizing packaging and handling processes, palletization enhances efficiency, reduces transit times, and minimizes the risk of damage or loss, thereby driving greater competitiveness and sustainability in global trade.

Topic 51: Stowage

Stowage is a critical aspect of maritime logistics, especially in the context of modern cargo vessels equipped to handle large volumes of goods efficiently. With the advent of palletization, unitization, and standardization, cargo ships have evolved to accommodate diverse cargo types while ensuring optimal distribution and stability.

The stowage process involves meticulous planning and arrangement of cargo within the vessel to maximize space utilization, minimize movement-induced damage, and ensure the safety of both the cargo and the vessel. This entails considering various factors such as cargo weight, volume, fragility, and environmental conditions.

Utilizing advanced Enterprise Resource Planning (ERP) systems and IT software, logistics professionals meticulously plan the stowage of cargo, taking into account the ship's layout, loading capacity, and handling equipment capabilities. The goal is to distribute the cargo strategically across different sections of the ship, such as the fore, amidships, and aft, to mitigate the effects of vessel movement and environmental elements.

Cargo that is susceptible to damage from exposure to elements like rain or stormwater is stowed below deck, shielded from external conditions. Additionally, cargo placement near the ship's center of gravity, particularly in the amidships section, helps minimize the impact of vessel movement and vibration, ensuring the stability of the cargo during transit.

While cargo stowed in the fore and aft sections may experience higher levels of movement and vibration, careful planning ensures that only cargo capable of withstanding such conditions is placed in these areas. By adhering to stowage best practices, logistics professionals optimize cargo distribution, enhance vessel stability, and mitigate the risk of damage or loss during transit.

Overall, effective stowage practices are essential for optimizing cargo handling operations, ensuring the safe and efficient transportation of goods by sea. Through meticulous planning and strategic cargo placement, logistics professionals uphold the integrity of the supply chain, facilitating the timely delivery of goods to their destination.

Topic 52: Benefits of Unitization and Palletization

Unitization and palletization bring numerous benefits to international trade and logistics, revolutionizing the movement of goods and enhancing operational efficiency. Let's delve into the key advantages:

Saving: Unitization and palletization enable significant cost savings in international logistics operations. By streamlining handling processes and optimizing freight transport, businesses can reduce costs associated with manual labor, handling equipment, and freight charges. Economies of scale further enhance savings, especially with large-scale operations.

Safety: With unitization and palletization, the safety of cargo is greatly enhanced. By consolidating goods into standardized units and pallets, the risk of damage or loss during handling and transport is minimized. Mechanized handling equipment ensures secure loading and unloading, reducing the likelihood of accidents and ensuring the integrity of the cargo.

Speed: One of the most significant benefits of unitization and palletization is the improvement in speed and efficiency. Mechanized operations, standardized processes, and unitized cargo enable swift handling and transport. With the support of IT systems, including automation and robotics, logistics operations become faster and more streamlined, facilitating timely delivery of goods.

Sustainability: Unitization and palletization contribute to sustainable logistics practices by optimizing resource utilization and reducing environmental impact. By maximizing cargo capacity and minimizing waste, businesses can achieve greater efficiency and reduce their carbon footprint. Smart logistics solutions, incorporating technologies like smart sensors, RFID tags, and artificial intelligence, further enhance sustainability efforts by enabling data-driven decision-making and resource optimization.

Overall, the adoption of unitization and palletization in international trade paves the way for smarter, more efficient logistics management. By leveraging standardized processes, mechanized handling, and advanced technologies, businesses can unlock new levels of cost-effectiveness, safety, speed, and sustainability in their logistics operations, driving greater competitiveness and success in the global market.

Topic 53: Containerization

Containerization stands as a monumental revolution in international logistics, transforming the way goods are transported across the globe. At its core, containerization involves the standardized packaging and shipment of goods within uniform containers. This practice stems from the principles of unitization, palletization, and standardization, streamlining the logistics process and enhancing efficiency.

These standardized containers, characterized by uniform shapes and sizes, are tailored for various modes of transportation, whether by sea or air. They provide a versatile solution for transporting manufactured goods, offering unparalleled convenience and reliability. While commodities or bulk cargo may not be ideal for containerization, it serves as a highly effective method for distributing a wide range of goods.

The impact of containerization reverberates throughout the international logistics industry, particularly in sea transportation. By optimizing and mechanizing cargo handling processes, containerization enables the seamless movement of large quantities of goods aboard massive ships. Moreover, it has revolutionized air transportation, facilitating the efficient handling of cargo with standardized air freight containers known as Unit Load Devices (ULDs).

Containers used in sea freight are typically classified based on size, with common variants including 20ft, 40ft, 45ft, 48ft, and 53ft containers. Among these, 40ft containers are the most prevalent in modern shipping operations, with 20ft containers also being widely utilized. Meanwhile, air freight containers, or ULDs, adhere to standardized dimensions to ensure compatibility with aircraft loading systems.

These containers serve diverse purposes, catering to the unique requirements of different types of cargo. From dry storage containers to flat rack containers, open top containers, and refrigerated ISO containers, each variant is designed to accommodate specific cargo types. Recent innovations, such as collapsible containers, continue to push the boundaries of containerization, offering new levels of flexibility and efficiency in the logistics landscape.

In essence, containerization epitomizes the convergence of

standardization, efficiency, and innovation in international logistics, driving unprecedented advancements in the movement of goods worldwide. By embracing this transformative approach, businesses can unlock new opportunities for cost-effectiveness, reliability, and sustainability in their logistics operations, fueling growth and competitiveness in the global marketplace.

Containerization has revolutionized the landscape of global trade, introducing standardized containers that streamline transportation processes and propel economic growth. These containers come in various types, each tailored to specific cargo requirements and transportation modes.

Dry storage containers are the most ubiquitous, commonly seen on trains, ships, and trucks, facilitating the transportation of a wide range of goods. Containers for heavy loads, characterized by their robust construction, ensure the secure transport of bulky items. Specialized containers, such as open-top and open-side storage containers, accommodate cargo that requires easy loading and unloading, while refrigerated ISO containers maintain the integrity of temperature-sensitive goods during transit. ISO tanks cater to the transportation of liquids, offering a secure and efficient solution for liquid cargo.

Half-height containers are ideal for transporting heavy materials like coal and stones, providing a compact and durable storage solution. Additionally, specialized containers designed for unique cargo requirements further enhance the versatility of containerization, catering to the diverse needs of the logistics industry.

The impact of containerization on global trade has been profound, significantly reducing loading and unloading times and lowering berthing times for ships at ports. Moreover, containerization has alleviated congestion at ports, paving the way for smoother operations and increased efficiency. The establishment of inland container depots (ICDs) and container freight stations (CFSs) has further bolstered the integrated international supply chain, facilitating seamless intermodal and multimodal transportation.

Containerization has revolutionized logistics management, enabling the safe and efficient passage of cargo across continents. Standardized container sizes and shapes have facilitated the mechanization of cargo handling processes, minimizing the risk of damage and theft while ensuring the safety of ground crews. This standardized approach to cargo handling has been instrumental in enhancing the overall safety and efficiency of global trade operations.

The transformative impact of containerization on global trade is evident in the rapid expansion of international trade volumes over the past five decades. With total world exports increasing more than 65 times, containerization has played a pivotal role in driving economic growth and fostering interconnectedness on a global scale. As international trade continues to evolve, containerization remains a cornerstone of modern logistics, driving efficiency, reliability, and prosperity in the global economy.

Topic 54: Chapter take away

In conclusion, the session has shed light on the pivotal role of unitization, palletization, and standardization in revolutionizing international logistics management. Without these foundational concepts, the modernization and mechanization of logistics operations would have been challenging to achieve. The need to reduce turnaround times for ships at ports necessitated optimized and standardized processes, which unitization and palletization facilitated effectively.

The substantial investments required to modernize logistics infrastructure, such as the development of state-of-the-art ports by companies like Dubai Ports (DP World) and the Adani Group in India, underscore the significance of these concepts. These investments are only feasible due to the efficiency gains brought about by unitization and palletization.

Looking ahead, the discussion on containerization promises to further illuminate the transformative impact of standardized containers on global trade. Containerization has ushered in a new era of efficiency, reliability, and connectivity in logistics, driving economic growth and fostering international trade.

In subsequent sessions, we will delve deeper into the intricacies of containerization and explore the profound implications it holds for the future of logistics and global commerce. Stay tuned as we continue to unravel the complexities and innovations shaping the landscape of international logistics management.

Chapter 9: Packing and Packaging

Topic 55: Chapter Overview

Welcome, everyone, to the next chapter focusing on an integral aspect of trade logistics: packing and packaging. In this session, we will delve into the fundamental concepts surrounding packing and packaging, exploring their definitions, distinctions, and significance in the realm of export shipments.

We will embark on a journey to understand the essential roles that packing and packaging play as protectors of goods traversing continents. Throughout our discussion, we will unravel the complexities of packaging, shedding light on its multifaceted purposes and the legal and regulatory compliances imperative for seamless global trade.

Furthermore, we will explore the rationale behind various types of packing and packaging, dissecting the factors that influence their selection and implementation in international trade scenarios. Join us as we navigate through the intricate landscape of packing and packaging in trade logistics, uncovering the strategies and considerations essential for efficient and secure shipment management.

Topic 56: Definition and significance

In the realm of international trade logistics, packing and packaging stand as the often overlooked yet indispensable guardians of the supply chain. Let's delve into the definition and significance of these crucial components in the seamless movement of goods across the globe.

Firstly, let's define packing and packaging. Packing involves the systematic arrangement of goods within containers, while packaging encompasses the materials and design used to protect and present these goods during transportation.

Now, why does proper packing and packaging matter in international logistics? Consider the journey your product undertakes across continents. From vibrations to shifts in temperature, numerous hazards await along the way. Proper packing and packaging act as the defenders, shielding your goods from these perils, especially during international transit.

Think of protection in transit. Sturdy boxes, cushioning materials, and secure seals form an armor against impact, moisture, and rough handling. Moreover, effective packaging extends the shelf life and preserves the quality of goods, crucial for perishable items destined for international markets.

Investing in proper packing and packaging mitigates risks, reducing damage or loss and minimizing financial losses and delays. It's an investment in the reliability and efficiency of your supply chain.

Furthermore, in this era of sustainability, packaging goes beyond protection. Embracing eco-friendly materials and practices not only safeguards goods but also minimizes environmental impact, aligning with global efforts towards a greener future.

In conclusion, packing and packaging aren't mere logistical components; they are the silent guardians of your products, ensuring their safe passage through the intricate web of global trade. Their significance lies not just in protection but in the assurance they provide—the integrity of your products, the trust of your overseas buyers, and the smooth flow of international commerce. Remember, how you pack and package isn't just about protection; it's a statement of commitment to quality, reliability, and sustainability in international logistics.

Topic 57: Need for packaging in trade logistics

In the realm of trade logistics, understanding the need for packaging is crucial as it impacts various logistics activities such as transportation, inventory management, warehousing, and communication. By analyzing the effects of different packaging strategies on these activities, we can identify trade-offs and make informed decisions to optimize the supply chain.

Table I. Packaging Cost Trade-Offs with Other Logistics Activities (Lambert et al., 1998).

Logistics activity	Trade-offs
Transportation	
Increased package information	Decreases shipment delays, increased package information decreases tracking of lost shipments
Increased package protection	Decreases damage and theft in transit, but increases package weight and transport costs.
Increased standardisation	Decreases handling costs, vehicle waiting time for loading and unloading; increased standardisation; increases modal choices for shipper and decreases need for specialised transport equipment
Inventory	
Increased product protection	Decreased theft, damage, insurance; increases product availability (sales); increases product value and carrying costs.
Warehousing	
Increased package information	Decreases order filling time, labour cost.
Increased product protection	Increases cube utilisation (stacking), but decreases cube utilisation by increasing the size of the product dimensions.
Increased standardisation	Decreases material handling equipment costs.
Communications	
Increased package information	Decreases other communications about the product such as telephone calls to track down lost shipments.

Starting with transportation, increasing packaging information leads to decreased shipping delays and reduces the time required for tracking lost shipments. However, enhancing package protection decreases damage and theft but results in increased package weight and transport costs. Similarly, standardizing packaging dimensions reduces handling costs, vehicle waiting time, and the need for specialized transport equipment.

Moving to inventory management, augmenting product protection decreases theft, damage, and insurance costs while increasing product availability and value. However, it also elevates product and transportation costs. In warehousing, enhanced product information reduces order filling time and labor costs. Increased product protection improves cube utilization for stacking but may decrease it due to larger product dimensions.

Finally, in communication, boosting packaging information decreases the need for additional communications to track lost shipments, thereby streamlining the process.

Understanding these impacts and trade-offs is essential for effective planning and decision-making in packing and packaging strategies. By carefully considering the effects on different logistics activities, businesses can optimize their supply chains for efficiency, cost-effectiveness, and reliability in international trade.

Topic 58: Levels and types of packaging

In international logistics, packaging plays a pivotal role in ensuring the safe and efficient movement of goods across continents. Understanding the levels and types of packaging is essential for optimizing the supply chain. Let's delve into this topic to grasp the intricacies of packaging in trade logistics.

Firstly, let's elucidate the three levels of packaging systems prevalent in international logistics. The primary packaging, also known as consumer or sales packaging, directly encases the product and is the packaging that consumers usually encounter and take home. Secondary packaging, on the other hand, groups several primary packages together, forming a larger unit for transportation and handling. Finally, tertiary packaging involves assembling primary or secondary packages onto pallets or roll containers, facilitating efficient storage, handling, and transport.

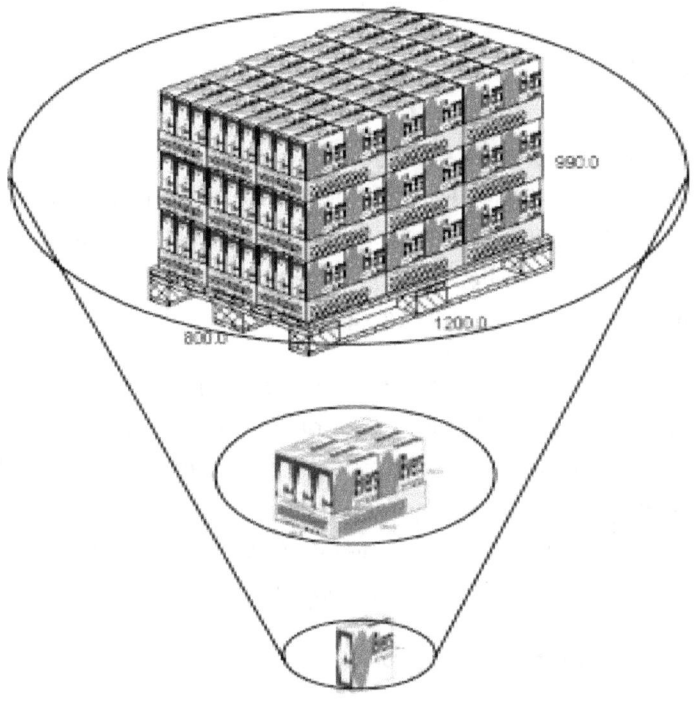

Packaging Type	Definition
Primary packaging, consumer packaging or sales packaging	Packaging which is in contact with the product. The packaging that the consumer usually takes home
Secondary packaging	Secondary packaging is designed to contain several primary packages
Tertiary packaging	Used when a number of primary or secondary packages are assembled on a pallet or roll container.
Group packaging	Packaging which is conceived to facilitate protection, display, handling and/or transport of a number of primary packages
Transport packaging, industrial packaging, or distribution packaging	Packaging which is conceived to facilitate handling, transport and storage of a number of primary packages in order to provide efficient production and distribution as well as prevent physical handling and transport damage
Display packaging	Same as group packaging, quite often with an emphasis on display features
Retail packaging	Same as group packaging with a special emphasis on the design to fit in retail
Used packaging	Packaging/packaging material remaining after the removal of the product it contained

Now, let's delve deeper into the various types of packaging. Primary packaging ensures the protection, display, and transportation of individual products. Secondary packaging, often termed group packaging, facilitates the handling and transport of multiple primary packages. Tertiary packaging, also known as transport, industrial, or distribution packaging, aims to prevent physical damage during handling and transportation, tailored to the specific characteristics of the goods being transported.

Other notable types of packaging include group packaging, designed to streamline handling and transport of primary packages; display packaging, emphasizing display features for retail environments; and retail packaging, optimized for retail display and consumer appeal. Additionally, used packaging refers to the material remaining after the removal of the product, highlighting the importance of sustainability and waste management in packaging practices.

Understanding these levels and types of packaging is crucial for efficient supply chain management in international trade. Each type serves a distinct purpose in safeguarding products, optimizing handling, and enhancing consumer appeal. By adopting appropriate packaging strategies, businesses can ensure the integrity of their products throughout the complex journey of global trade.

Topic 59: Role and rationale of packaging in trade logistics

In the realm of international trade logistics, packaging serves as a critical component, influencing various facets of the supply chain. Let's explore the role and rationale of packaging in trade logistics to comprehend its significance in ensuring seamless operations and customer satisfaction.

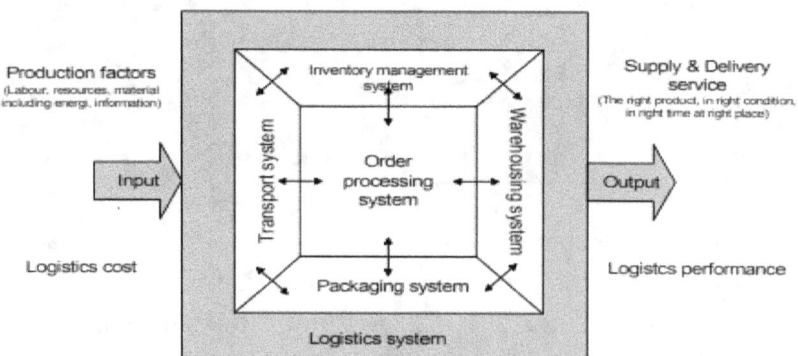

Packaging plays a pivotal role as one of the fundamental elements in the logistics system. It serves as an input factor, encompassing various production factors such as labor, resources, materials (including energy), and crucial product information. These factors collectively contribute to the logistics costs, thus highlighting the importance of efficient packaging practices in cost optimization.

Within the logistics system, packaging functions as one of the essential pillars alongside inventory management, transport, and warehousing systems. Together, these components interact synergistically with the order processing system, forming a cohesive diamond model of logistics. This model illustrates how these interconnected elements work in harmony to drive logistics performance and deliver optimal supply and delivery services.

The packaging system, as depicted in the model, plays a pivotal role in ensuring the integrity and safety of products throughout the supply chain journey. By utilizing appropriate packaging materials, designs, and labeling techniques, businesses can enhance product protection, minimize transportation risks, and streamline handling processes.

Ultimately, the effectiveness of the packaging system directly contributes to the logistics performance, enabling the timely and accurate delivery of products to customers. A well-designed and executed packaging strategy ensures that the right products reach the right destinations in optimal conditions, thereby bolstering customer satisfaction and loyalty.

In summary, the role of packaging in trade logistics is indispensable, serving as a linchpin in the efficient functioning of the supply chain. By recognizing the significance of packaging and adopting strategic approaches to packaging design and implementation, businesses can unlock numerous benefits, including cost savings, risk mitigation, and enhanced customer experiences.

Topic 60: Types of hazards associated with packing and transportation

Understanding the various hazards associated with packing and transportation is paramount in ensuring the safe and secure delivery of goods across the supply chain. Let's delve into the different types of transit hazards that packaging must address to mitigate risks effectively.

Firstly, shock poses a significant risk, often resulting from drops or impacts during handling processes. To safeguard against shock-related damage, packaging must provide adequate cushioning and protection to absorb and dissipate the impact forces.

Secondly, vibrations encountered during transportation journeys can also pose a threat to the integrity of packaged goods. To counteract this hazard, packaging solutions should be designed to minimize the transmission of vibrations and prevent potential damage to fragile items.

Compression hazards arise when packages are stacked in storage facilities or vehicles, exerting pressure on the contents. Effective packaging strategies involve selecting materials and designs capable of withstanding compression forces and maintaining the structural integrity of the packaged goods.

Lastly, atmospheric hazards encompass various environmental factors such as temperature fluctuations, humidity levels, altitude changes, and static electricity. Packaging must be engineered to shield products from these atmospheric elements, ensuring their preservation and quality throughout the transportation process.

By addressing these four categories of transport hazards through appropriate packaging solutions, businesses can minimize the risk of damage, spoilage, and loss during transit. Implementing robust packaging strategies tailored to mitigate these hazards is essential for safeguarding product integrity and enhancing customer satisfaction in the global trade logistics landscape.

Topic 61: Regulatory compliance in packaging for global trade

Navigating the regulatory landscape in packaging for global trade is a critical aspect of international logistics that often operates behind the scenes. Let's delve into the world of regulatory compliance and understand its paramount importance in ensuring seamless global trade.

International regulations and standards governing packaging materials and practices form an intricate tapestry of global commerce. Bodies such as the International Organization for Standardization (ISO) and regional authorities impose guidelines to ensure safety, environmental sustainability, and product integrity during international transportation across all modes.

These regulations cover a wide spectrum of aspects, ranging from material specifications to design requirements, handling, and disposal guidelines. Crafted to safeguard products, the environment, and consumer well-being, compliance with these regulations is crucial for global trade.

Imagine shipping goods to diverse destinations worldwide, each with its own packaging regulations. Non-compliance could lead to rejected shipments, customs delays, or hefty penalties. Adhering to these regulations mitigates such risks, ensuring smoother, uninterrupted trade flows.

Navigating the compliance landscape may seem daunting, but it is imperative. Familiarizing oneself with regulations pertinent to different regions and industries becomes pivotal. These regulations encompass diverse aspects, including material usage, product labeling, recyclability symbols, and hazardous substance restrictions.

Standards play a crucial role in achieving compliance. Adhering to recognized standards ensures conformity and signifies a commitment to quality and safety. ISO standards offer comprehensive guidelines for packaging, fostering smoother cross-border trade practices aligned with global norms.

In the realm of international logistics, ensuring compliance is a strategic imperative. Engaging with regulatory bodies, staying updated with evolving standards, and integrating compliance checks into supply chain processes are essential. Collaboration with packaging experts and industry peers aids in navigating the maze of regulations, ensuring seamless trade operations.

Topic 62: Concluding remarks

In conclusion, packaging plays a crucial role in the intricate web of global trade logistics. From protecting goods during transit to ensuring regulatory compliance, packaging serves as a silent yet indispensable component of international commerce.

Throughout this chapter, we've explored various aspects of packaging, including its definition, significance, types, hazards, and regulatory compliance. We've delved into the rationale behind different packaging practices, understanding how they contribute to the efficiency and reliability of supply chains worldwide.

We've learned about the importance of regulatory compliance in packaging for global trade, recognizing the necessity of adhering to international standards and regulations to facilitate seamless cross-border transactions.

As we navigate the complexities of international logistics, it becomes evident that proper packaging is not just about protecting products; it's about ensuring consumer safety, environmental sustainability, and the integrity of global trade networks.

By embracing best practices in packaging and staying updated with evolving regulations and standards, businesses can mitigate risks, enhance efficiency, and foster smoother trade operations across continents.

In essence, packaging serves as a silent guardian of goods, ensuring their safe passage through the intricate channels of global commerce. As we move forward, let us continue to recognize the pivotal role of packaging in shaping the future of international trade logistics.

Chapter 10: Choosing the right material for packaging in international trade logistics

Topic 63: Chapter Overview

Welcome to the new section on choosing the right material for packaging in international trade logistics. In the previous section, we delved into the intricacies of packing and packaging, understanding their significance in the realm of global commerce. Now, we venture further to explore the critical aspect of selecting the appropriate packaging material.

Throughout this section, we will uncover the importance of material selection in packaging for international trade logistics. Understanding the significance of choosing the right material goes beyond just cost considerations; it encompasses regulatory compliance, environmental sustainability, and meeting the evolving challenges of the industry.

Our journey will take us through various objectives of packaging, factors to consider when selecting materials, and the different types of packing materials commonly used in international trade logistics. We will explore the consequences of not choosing the right material and discuss the major functions of an ideal package.

Moreover, we will delve into the urgent need for sustainable packaging, examining why it has become a critical aspect of international trade logistics and exploring solutions and examples from the industry.

By the end of this section, you will gain a comprehensive understanding of the diverse materials available for packaging in international trade logistics and the crucial role they play in ensuring the efficiency, safety, and sustainability of global supply chains. So, let's embark on this journey to enhance our knowledge and understanding of packaging materials in the context of international trade logistics.

Topic 64: Objectives of a typical packaging efforts

In this section, we delve into the objectives of packaging efforts in international trade logistics. As marketers, our primary goal is to ensure a delightful unboxing experience for customers, leaving a lasting impression that goes beyond mere protection of goods. This experience not only attracts new customers but also fosters loyalty among existing ones.

Moreover, packaging plays a crucial role in conveying our commitment to environmental sustainability and regulatory compliance, addressing concerns that resonate with customers worldwide. Ensuring the protection of goods throughout their international journey is paramount, requiring careful consideration of factors such as mode of transportation, product characteristics, and atmospheric conditions.

Topic 65: Factors to consider when choosing material for packaging

Budgetary constraints, strength requirements, and the expectations of overseas buyers also influence the choice of packaging material. By aligning packaging objectives with business goals and customer expectations, we can enhance brand value and facilitate smooth transportation and clearance of goods.

Factors to Consider when **Choosing a Packaging Material**

⌐ Mode of transportation	⌐ Moisture	⌐ Characteristics of the products	⌐ Size of the products
⌐ Temperature	⌐ Budget	⌐ Strength of the material	⌐ Business audience

As we explore the factors to consider when choosing the right packaging material, we aim to equip ourselves with the knowledge needed to make informed decisions that optimize efficiency, sustainability, and customer satisfaction in international trade logistics. Let's navigate through these considerations to ensure the success of our packaging efforts in the global marketplace.

Topic 66: Types of materials commonly used in tertiary packaging

In international trade logistics, a variety of packaging materials are commonly used to ensure the safe transportation of goods. These materials cater to different needs and preferences, offering a range of options to suit various products and shipping requirements.

One commonly used material is wooden boxes, known for their durability and strength. These boxes provide robust protection for goods during transit, making them ideal for heavy or delicate items.

Corrugated boxes or boards are another popular choice, valued for their versatility and affordability. These lightweight yet sturdy containers offer excellent cushioning and stacking capabilities, making them suitable for a wide range of products.

Plywood crates are preferred for their strength and resilience, particularly for items requiring extra protection against impact or rough handling. These crates provide a reliable solution for shipping heavy or irregularly shaped goods.

Steel-based packaging offers unparalleled durability and security, making it ideal for high-value or hazardous items. While relatively heavier and more expensive, steel containers provide exceptional protection against external threats.

Plastics are widely used in various forms, including containers, wraps, and bags, offering flexibility, moisture resistance, and cost-effectiveness. Plastic packaging is versatile and can be tailored to specific product requirements, making it a popular choice across industries.

Additionally, jute-based packaging emerges as an environmentally friendly option, appreciated for its biodegradability and sustainability. Jute containers and bags provide an eco-conscious alternative for packaging, contributing to reduced environmental impact.

Moreover, ongoing innovation in packaging materials introduces new possibilities and solutions. Recycled materials and innovative designs continue to enter the market, offering sustainable alternatives and addressing emerging challenges in international trade logistics.

By understanding the diverse range of packaging materials available, businesses can make informed decisions to optimize packaging solutions for their specific needs and contribute to efficient and sustainable global trade.

Topic 67: What is at stake?

Choosing the right material for packaging in international trade logistics is critical, as the consequences of making mistakes can be significant. Understanding what is at stake underscores the importance of meticulous decision-making in this aspect of business operations.

At stake is the safety of the products being transported. Inadequate packaging materials can jeopardize the integrity of goods, leading to damage, loss, or contamination during transit. This not only affects the quality of the products but also impacts customer satisfaction and trust.

Furthermore, the reputation of the company is on the line. Poor packaging choices can tarnish the image of the business, eroding customer confidence and loyalty. A company's brand equity and market position are closely tied to its ability to deliver products safely and reliably.

The entire business model may be at risk if packaging materials are not chosen wisely. Supply chain disruptions, delays, and additional costs arising from packaging-related issues can undermine the efficiency and profitability of the business.

Commercial aspects of the business, including sales, revenue, and profitability, are also impacted. Damage or loss of goods due to inadequate packaging can lead to financial losses, insurance claims, and potential legal liabilities, affecting the bottom line of the company.

Moreover, environmental considerations come into play. Sustainable packaging practices are increasingly important in today's global trade landscape, with regulations and consumer preferences driving the demand for eco-friendly solutions. Failing to adopt environmentally responsible packaging materials can result in negative environmental impact and reputational damage.

Compliance with local and international regulations is essential. Packaging materials must meet regulatory standards to ensure safety, security, and environmental sustainability. Non-compliance can result in legal penalties, customs delays, or rejection of shipments, disrupting business operations and relationships with trading partners.

Lastly, the goods of other suppliers are also at stake. In the interconnected world of international trade, problems with one shipment can have ripple effects, affecting neighboring shipments and suppliers. Ensuring the integrity and safety of packaging materials is crucial to safeguarding the interests of all stakeholders involved in the global supply chain.

Topic 68: 5 major functions of ideal packaging

The five major functions of ideal packaging play a crucial role in ensuring the success of international trade logistics. Let's delve into each of these functions to understand their significance:

Protection: The primary function of packaging is to safeguard the goods during their journey in international trade. Ideal packaging materials and designs offer protection against various hazards such as impacts, vibrations, compression, and atmospheric conditions, ensuring the integrity and quality of the products remain intact.

Identification: In the vast sea of goods transported through international trade channels, proper identification is essential. Ideal packaging enables easy identification of the goods, both on board and off board vessels, in warehouses, and during customs clearance. Clear labeling and marking facilitate smooth handling by intermediaries and customs departments, streamlining the logistics process.

Communication: Effective communication through packaging is vital for ensuring safety and compliance with regulations. Proper labeling and markings communicate critical information about the contents of the package, including any hazardous materials or special handling instructions. Honest and accurate communication instills confidence in handlers and ensures regulatory compliance throughout the supply chain.

Convenience: Ideal packaging prioritizes convenience for all stakeholders involved in the logistics process. From manufacturers to port handlers, intermediaries, and customs officials, packaging should be easy to handle, transport, and store. Convenience enhances efficiency, reduces the risk of errors, and promotes smoother operations across the supply chain.

Marketing: Packaging serves as a powerful marketing tool even during transit. An ideal package effectively promotes the brand, company, and product, reinforcing marketing strategies throughout the journey. Eye-catching designs, branding elements, and product information on the packaging contribute to brand visibility and recognition, enhancing the overall marketing impact.

By fulfilling these five functions effectively, ideal packaging contributes to the success of international trade logistics, ensuring product safety, regulatory compliance, operational efficiency, and brand promotion throughout the supply chain.

Topic 69: Common materials used in primary packaging and need for sustainable packaging

In the realm of packaging, various materials play a significant role, serving different functions across primary, secondary, and tertiary packing. Common materials used include plastics, metals, papers, foils, aluminum foils, glass, and more. These materials are employed in diverse forms to ensure the safety, identification, communication, and convenience of goods during transit.

However, the reliance on traditional packaging materials has led to environmental concerns, with packaging materials contributing to approximately 65% of global solid waste. The staggering figures reveal the pressing need for sustainable packaging solutions.

To address this issue, innovative materials are emerging in the market, offering eco-friendly alternatives to conventional packaging. Sustainable packaging aims to minimize environmental impact by reducing waste generation, promoting recycling, and utilizing biodegradable materials.

The urgency for sustainable packaging is evident in the alarming statistics surrounding plastic production and waste management. Approximately 380 million tons of plastics are produced annually worldwide, with only a small fraction being recycled or incinerated. The majority of plastic waste ends up polluting land and oceans, posing serious threats to ecosystems and human health.

In the context of international trade logistics, the need for sustainable packaging is paramount. Given the significant contribution of packaging materials to global solid waste, the logistics industry must prioritize environmentally friendly practices. By adopting sustainable packaging solutions, businesses can minimize their environmental footprint and contribute to a healthier, more sustainable future.

Topic 70: Solutions, examples and discussion questions

In addressing the pressing need for sustainable packaging solutions, several strategies and examples offer valuable insights and potential avenues for improvement.

One solution lies in the exploration and adoption of innovative materials that are biodegradable, compostable, and preferably plant-based. By leveraging advancements in packaging design, businesses can optimize material usage and enhance sustainability. Furthermore, improvements in distribution methods and the extension of material lifespan through reuse initiatives contribute to a more environmentally friendly approach.

A compelling case study from Coca-Cola demonstrates the power of incorporating sustainability messages into branding efforts. In Sweden,

Coca-Cola labels advocate for a circular economy by urging consumers to recycle their plastic bottles. The campaign, featuring simple yet impactful messages like "Recycle me again," emphasizes the recyclability of Coca-Cola's bottles and encourages ongoing reuse. Such initiatives not only align with environmental goals but also strengthen brand identity and consumer engagement.

THE *Coca-Cola* COMPANY

Coca-Cola Labels in Sweden Issue Call to Action in Support of a Circular Economy
'Recycle Me Again: I Am Made of 100% Recycled Plastic'

As we reflect on these examples, several discussion questions arise:

How effective would similar campaigns be if introduced in your country?

What strategies could be implemented to enhance the effectiveness of sustainability messaging?

Are there any barriers or challenges that may hinder the success of such initiatives in your country?

What role should government entities play in supporting and incentivizing sustainable practices within the industry?

By engaging with these questions, we can gain deeper insights into the feasibility and impact of sustainability initiatives within the packaging industry and explore avenues for collaborative action towards a more sustainable future.

Topic 71: Innovative ideas for primary packing - Idea 1

Introducing an innovative solution poised to revolutionize the packaging industry: the edible water bubble. Developed by Skipping Rocks Lab, this groundbreaking product aims to replace traditional plastic bottles with a natural and biodegradable alternative made from seaweed.

The edible water bubble, known as Oho, offers a sustainable solution for hydration on the go, ideal for events like festivals, marathons, and everyday use. Unlike plastic bottles, Oho is not only biodegradable but also edible, addressing concerns about plastic waste and environmental impact.

Skipping Rocks Lab has invested years in developing this technology, refining the properties of the seaweed-based membrane to ensure its effectiveness and affordability. With successful pilot events and positive reception from consumers, the company is now poised to scale up production and bring Oho to larger audiences, targeting major events such as the London Marathon and Glastonbury.

Behind this innovative endeavor is a dedicated team of chemists, engineers, and business professionals committed to driving positive change in the packaging industry. Led by experienced individuals with backgrounds in finance, engineering, and product design, Skipping Rocks Lab is poised to lead the charge towards a more sustainable future.

To support their mission and be part of the movement to reduce plastic waste, Skipping Rocks Lab is inviting individuals to invest in their vision. Through shares starting as low as £10, investors can contribute to the company's growth and be part of the journey towards a more sustainable and eco-friendly packaging solution.

Innovative ideas like the edible water bubble demonstrate the potential for creativity and ingenuity to address pressing environmental challenges and pave the way for a more sustainable future.

Topic 72: More ideas and section take away

In our exploration of innovative packaging solutions, we've uncovered some truly inspiring ideas that are shaping the future of sustainable packaging.

One such example is LOLIWARE, a company pioneering the use of AI-driven seaweed biomaterials as an eco-friendly alternative to traditional plastics. Their revolutionary approach holds promise for reducing plastic waste and minimizing environmental impact.

Additionally, L'oreal's collaboration with Paboco has led to the development of paper bottles, offering a sustainable solution for packaging beauty products. This innovative endeavor highlights the potential for creative partnerships to drive positive change in the industry.

As we reflect on these examples, it becomes clear that the choices we make in packaging materials have far-reaching implications for the environment, society, and our businesses. By embracing innovative solutions and rethinking traditional practices, we can pave the way for a more sustainable future.

In conclusion, this section has provided valuable insights into the importance of selecting the right packaging materials and the role they play in addressing environmental concerns. By understanding the philosophy behind packaging and its functional aspects, we can make informed decisions that benefit both our businesses and the planet.

Thank you for joining me on this journey of exploration and discovery. Together, let's continue to champion sustainability and make a positive impact through our packaging choices.

Concluding remarks

As we draw to a close on this chapter, it's evident that the world of packaging in international trade logistics is undergoing a transformative shift towards sustainability and innovation. Throughout our discussion, we've delved into the crucial role of packaging materials, explored innovative solutions, and highlighted the importance of considering environmental concerns.

By understanding the objectives of packaging, the types of materials commonly used, and the need for sustainable alternatives, we've gained valuable insights into the evolving landscape of packaging practices. From edible water bubbles to AI-driven seaweed biomaterials, the possibilities for sustainable packaging solutions are both inspiring and diverse.

As businesses and individuals, we have a responsibility to make informed choices that prioritize environmental sustainability while meeting the demands of global trade logistics. By embracing innovative ideas, collaborating with industry partners, and adhering to regulatory standards, we can pave the way for a more sustainable future.

In closing, let us continue to explore, innovate, and advocate for sustainable packaging practices that benefit both our businesses and the planet. Together, we can create a more sustainable and resilient global trade ecosystem for generations to come. Thank you for your engagement and commitment to sustainability in international trade logistics.

Chapter 11: Marking And Labeling

Topic 73: Chapter Overview

In this chapter, we delve into the crucial aspects of marking and labeling in export shipments, essential for the smooth movement of cargo across international borders. Building on our understanding of packaging materials from the previous section, we now turn our attention to the significance and importance of marking and labeling.

Marking and labeling play a pivotal role in creating the ideal package, encompassing various dimensions such as design, material, size, and dimensions. Throughout this section, we will explore the diverse objectives of marking and labeling, providing context to the topic and facilitating a deeper understanding of its importance.

Starting with an examination of the objectives, we'll uncover how marking and labeling contribute to package identification, compliance with House Air Way Bills and Master Air Way Bills, handling of hazardous or special cargo, meeting importers' requirements, adhering to local regulations, and addressing intellectual property rights concerns.

By navigating through these different objectives, we aim to illuminate the crucial role and significance of marking and labeling in international trade logistics. Join us as we unravel the complexities and nuances of this essential aspect of cargo movement across borders. Let's embark on this journey together and gain valuable insights into the world of marking and labeling in export shipments.

Topic 74: Understanding objectives of marking and labeling

In this section, we delve into the various objectives of marking and labeling, providing a comprehensive understanding of their significance in international trade logistics. Let's begin by exploring the primary objectives:

Package Identification: The foremost objective is to ensure clear and accurate identification of packages. This involves labeling shipments with information essential for tracking and managing cargo throughout its journey. We'll delve deeper into this aspect to understand its importance and practical implementation.

House AWB and Master AWB: We'll address the challenge posed by House Air Waybills (AWBs) issued by intermediaries, distinct from the Master AWBs issued by carriers. Understanding how markings and labeling facilitate the management of this dichotomy is crucial for smooth cargo movement.

Communication and Handling of Hazardous Cargo: Handling hazardous cargo requires clear communication and appropriate labeling to ensure the safety of goods, personnel, and the environment. We'll discuss how effective markings and labeling mitigate risks associated with hazardous materials and special handling requirements.

Importer's Requirements: Importers may have specific requirements regarding markings and labeling for customs clearance and compliance. We'll explore how understanding and meeting these requirements are essential for successful international trade transactions.

Compliance with Regulations: Local and international regulations mandate specific markings and labeling standards to ensure regulatory compliance. We'll examine how adherence to these standards is crucial for avoiding delays, penalties, and legal issues in cross-border trade.

Intellectual Property Rights (IPR) Concerns: Markings and labeling play a vital role in protecting intellectual property rights, such as trademarks, copyrights, and patents. We'll discuss how effective labeling strategies help safeguard against counterfeiting and unauthorized use of branded products.

By addressing these objectives, we aim to equip you with the knowledge and insights necessary to navigate the complexities of marking and labeling in international trade logistics effectively. Let's delve into each objective to understand its implications and practical applications in the global marketplace.

Topic 75: Role in Package Identification

In this section, we focus on the pivotal role of markings in package identification within the realm of international trade logistics. Markings serve as crucial identifiers for shipments and cargo, facilitating seamless tracking and management throughout the supply chain.

As we discussed earlier, an ideal package encompasses various functions, with package identification being paramount. Markings fulfill this role by providing clear and standardized identifiers for shipments and cargo. These markings, present on all packages within a shipment, are replicated on essential documents like packing lists.

The packing list, a vital document accompanying shipments, plays a pivotal role in ensuring accurate package identification. It serves as a reference point for the markings, ensuring they are correctly documented and replicated. This meticulous attention to detail ensures smooth handling and tracking of cargo throughout its journey.

While markings may appear on various packaging levels, such as primary and secondary packaging, they are particularly essential on tertiary packaging. Tertiary packaging, comprising pallets or groupings of packages, requires clear and visible markings for efficient handling and loading into containers.

In the subsequent sections, we will delve deeper into the practical aspects of marking and labeling, exploring their significance in various shipment documents and processes. By understanding the role of markings in package identification, you will gain valuable insights into optimizing logistical operations and ensuring the integrity of shipments. Let's explore further to enhance our understanding of this critical aspect of international trade logistics.

Topic 76: Role in Solving the House Air Way Bill Problem

In the context of the House Air Way Bill (AWB) and the Master AWB, exporters often encounter a logistical challenge. While the carrier issues the Master AWB, exporters typically deal with intermediaries like forwarders or agents, resulting in the issuance of a House AWB.

However, markings play a pivotal role in resolving this discrepancy. Despite the differences between House AWB and Master AWB, markings serve as a universal identifier across both documents. Whether it's the House AWB or the Master AWB, the markings remain consistent, providing a common platform for communication and documentation.

Consider the scenario where the exporter hands over the cargo to the forwarder, who subsequently issues the House AWB before transferring the cargo to the carrier. The carrier then issues the Master AWB. This process involves a time gap, during which the House AWB serves as a temporary solution.

Markings bridge this gap effectively, ensuring seamless communication and coordination between all parties involved. By maintaining consistency in markings across both AWBs, exporters can navigate the complexities of international trade logistics with confidence and efficiency. Thus, marking emerges as a fundamental tool in overcoming the challenges associated with the House Air Way Bill problem.

Topic 77: Role in handling hazardous material shipments

When it comes to handling hazardous materials or dangerous goods in export shipments, the role of marking is paramount. Markings serve as a comprehensive identifier, encompassing descriptive names, identification numbers, instructions, and cautionary information specific to the hazardous material being transported.

Essentially, markings communicate critical details such as the weight quantity, specifications, and United Nations marks associated with the cargo. These UN marks, represented by different numbers indicating the severity of danger, must be prominently displayed through labels on the outer packaging of hazardous materials or dangerous goods.

It's crucial to distinguish between marking and labeling in this context. While marking pertains to the descriptive information directly applied to the packaging, labeling involves the display of international marks and labels, such as UN marks, on the packaging.

Correctly adhering to marking requirements ensures compliance with international regulations governing the transportation of hazardous materials. While handling hazardous materials entails additional costs, adherence to marking standards is non-negotiable, ensuring the safe and lawful transport of goods across borders.

Topic 78: How to implement correct markings

Implementing correct markings is essential for ensuring compliance with international regulations and facilitating the smooth movement of cargo. Here's what you need to know about implementing correct markings:

Durability: Markings must be durable to withstand the rigors of transportation and handling.

Language: Markings should be in the English language, as it is universally understood in international business.

Placement: Markings must be printed on or affixed to the surface of a package, label, tag, or sign.

Contrasting Colors: Markings should be displayed on a background of sharply contrasting colors to ensure ease of reading. If necessary, use colored paper to create a suitable background.

Unobscured Display: Markings should not be obscured by labels or attachments. They must be clearly visible and unobstructed.

Location: Markings should be located away from any other markings that are not essential for compliance. Priority should be given to core markings related to operations rather than marketing or branding.

By adhering to these guidelines, you can effectively implement correct markings on your packaging, ensuring compliance with regulations and efficient handling of cargo during transportation.

Topic 79: Role of specialized markings

Specialized markings play a crucial role in ensuring the safe handling and transportation of certain goods, especially hazardous or dangerous materials. Here's why specialized markings are important:

Package orientation

Package Orientation: For liquids, hazardous, or dangerous goods, package orientation markings are essential. These markings indicate the correct orientation of the package to prevent spills or leaks during transit.

Specific Hazardous Materials: Different categories of hazardous materials, such as radioactive or poisonous substances, require specific markings to convey their nature accurately. These markings help handlers identify and handle the goods safely.

HAZARDOUS MATERIALS MARKINGS

Clear Communication: Specialized markings communicate important information about the contents of the package, such as potential hazards or handling instructions. This ensures that everyone involved in the transportation process is aware of any risks and knows how to handle the goods appropriately.

Compliance: Compliance with specialized marking requirements is often mandated by regulations to ensure the safety of both workers and the environment. Properly marked packages are more likely to meet regulatory standards and avoid delays or penalties during transportation.

Resource Availability: Comprehensive lists of specialized hazardous material markings are available for reference, providing guidance on the correct symbols and labels to use for different types of goods. Access to these resources ensures that markings are accurate and compliant with industry standards.

By prioritizing the use of specialized markings and adhering to regulatory requirements, businesses can mitigate risks associated with the transportation of hazardous materials and promote safety throughout the supply chain.

Topic 80: All about export goods labeling

Export goods labeling serves the critical function of identifying specific hazards associated with the goods being transported. Here's what you need to know about export goods labeling:

Identifying Hazards: The primary purpose of labeling is to clearly identify the hazards present in the shipment. This is achieved through the use of specific colors, codes, and pictograms that indicate the type of materials and the nature of the hazard they pose.

Distinguishing from Marking: Unlike marking, which focuses on basic identification, labeling provides more detailed information. Labels often use multi-color designs, codes, and pictograms to convey a deeper understanding of the hazards associated with the goods.

UN Hazard Classes: Understanding the United Nations hazard classes is crucial for proper labeling. These classes cover a wide range of hazards, including explosives, flammable substances, corrosive materials, radioactive substances, and more. Each class has specific requirements for labeling.

Standard Labels: Hazardous materials warning labels adhere to standard formats and designs. They must be affixed to packages in a clear and prominent manner to ensure that handlers and authorities can easily identify the associated hazards.

Ensuring Safety: Warning labels serve as a vital communication tool, alerting everyone involved in the transportation process to potential dangers. Whether it's warehouse staff, customs officials, or transport personnel, clear labeling helps ensure the safe handling and storage of hazardous goods.

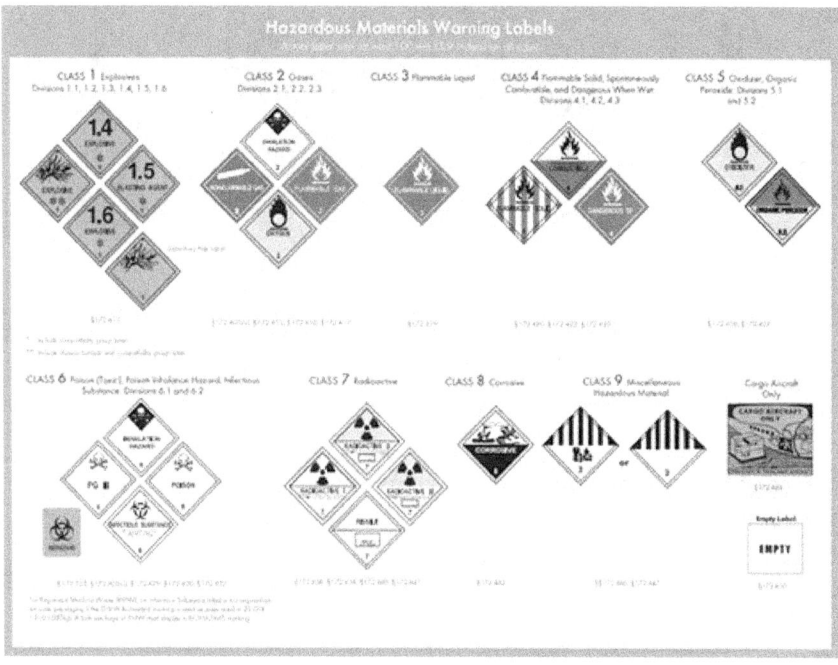

By following standard labeling practices and understanding the UN hazard classes, exporters can effectively communicate the risks associated with their goods and promote safety throughout the supply chain. For a comprehensive list of UN hazard classes and labeling requirements, refer to the provided document in the source section.

Topic 81: Understanding shipping markings

Understanding shipping markings is essential for efficient operations and proper handling of cargo. Here's what you need to know:

Shipping Marks Guide: While not mandatory, a shipping marks guide provides valuable guidance for marking packages effectively. These marks serve operational purposes and should be distinct from less important labels used for marketing or branding. Typically, shipping marks are in black color against a brown background, ensuring clear visibility.

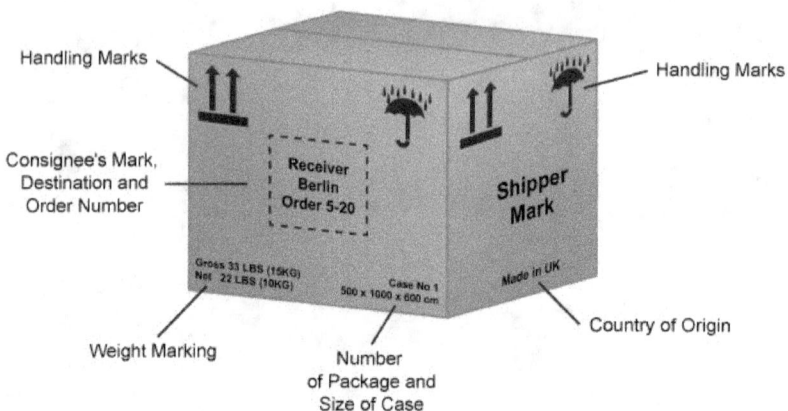

Types of Marks: The guide includes various types of marks, each serving a specific purpose. These may include handling marks, consignee's marks, destination and order numbers, weight markings, number of packages, size of the case, country of origin, and special handling marks.

Proper Placement: The guide outlines the ideal placement and proportions for each type of mark. This ensures consistency and clarity in communication across shipments. For example, if the cargo is liquid, orientation marks indicating the correct position may be necessary.

Special Handling Marks: Special handling marks communicate specific instructions for handling the cargo. These marks may indicate fragile items, orientation requirements, protection from moisture, or other special considerations. Unlike warning labels, special handling marks are simpler in design and often displayed in black or red color.

CARGO MARKING
(handling marks)

Resource Availability: A comprehensive list of handling marks is available for download in the resource section of this lecture. This resource provides valuable guidance on how to mark packages effectively to facilitate smooth handling and transportation.

By adhering to proper shipping marking practices and utilizing the provided guide, exporters can ensure that their cargo is handled correctly throughout the shipping process. Clear and consistent markings contribute to operational efficiency and help prevent mishandling or damage during transit.

Topic 82: Understanding typical requirements of markings and labeling by an importer

Understanding the typical requirements of markings and labeling by an importer is crucial for smooth import operations and compliance with local regulations. Here's what you need to know:

Business Requirements: Importers may have specific business requirements for markings and labeling, such as including their logo, address, or license information on packages. These requirements may be mandatory or dictated by local regulations in the importing country.

Local Regulations: Customs authorities in different countries may mandate certain markings and labeling on imported goods. For example, Indian customs regulations require specific information on packages intended for sale in the domestic market. This includes the importer's name and address, generic commodity names, net quantity in metric units, and the month and year of packing.

Maximum Retail Price (MRP): In India, packaged goods intended for retail sale must display the maximum retail price, which includes all applicable charges and taxes. Additionally, goods not meant for retail sale must be clearly labeled as such.

Labeling Requirements: Imported packaged food products must adhere to labeling requirements set forth by regulations such as the Prevention of Food Adulteration (PFA) rules of 1955 and the Packaged Commodities Rules of 1977 in India. These requirements include listing ingredients, manufacturer information, country of origin, net weight, batch or lot numbers, manufacturing and expiry dates, and MRP.

Additional Information: Depending on the product type, additional labeling requirements may apply. For example, symbols indicating the irradiation status of food products or distinguishing between vegetarian and non-vegetarian items are necessary in India due to cultural sensitivities.

Compliance with Standards: Importers must ensure that all markings and labeling comply with local standards and regulations, such as those governing food products. Non-compliance can lead to delays in customs clearance or even rejection of the imported goods.

By understanding and adhering to the specific requirements for markings and labeling imposed by the importing country, importers can ensure compliance, avoid regulatory issues, and facilitate the smooth entry of their goods into the market.

Topic 83: IPR concerns and section take away

In the final part of this chapter, let's delve into the critical topic of intellectual property rights (IPR) concerns and wrap up our discussion on markings and labeling.

Plaintiffs' label   Defendants' old label

Role of Labeling in IPR Protection: Labeling plays a crucial role in protecting intellectual property rights. It ensures that brands can distinguish themselves in the market and prevent confusion among consumers. For example, we discussed a case where two brands had similar labels, leading to legal disputes over brand identity and product differentiation.

Importance of Label Protection: Labels are valuable assets for companies, representing their brand identity, reputation, and market positioning. It's essential to safeguard labels through legal means to prevent unauthorized use and maintain brand integrity.

Key Takeaways: Throughout this section, we've explored various aspects of marking and labeling, including their significance in communicating product information, ensuring safety in handling hazardous materials, and complying with international standards and local regulations. By understanding the importance of marking and labeling, businesses can enhance their packaging practices, protect their brands, and ensure compliance with legal requirements.

In conclusion, mastering the art of marking and labeling is essential for businesses engaged in international trade. It not only facilitates the smooth movement of goods but also safeguards brand identity and ensures compliance with regulations. Thank you for exploring this crucial aspect of packaging with us.

Chapter 12: Surface and Sea Transportation

Topic 84: Chapter Overview

Welcome to the next section focusing on surface and sea transportation. In our previous discussions, we delved into the intricacies of packing and packaging, providing you with a comprehensive understanding of these crucial aspects. Now, we shift our focus to surface and sea transportation, pivotal components in the global movement of goods.

Surface and sea transportation play a paramount role in international trade, serving as the primary modes for transporting goods across vast distances. In this section, we will explore the various modes of surface transportation, including railways, roadways, and waterways. Additionally, we will delve into the realm of sea transportation, examining different vessel types, sizes, and operational dynamics.

Why are surface and sea transportation so significant? Simply put, they offer a cost-effective and efficient means of transporting bulk cargo internationally. As we navigate through this section, we will uncover the intricacies of these transportation modes, shedding light on the operations of shipping companies, the types of vessels they employ, and the contractual arrangements with shippers.

Surface transportation encompasses railways, roadways, waterways, and even pipelines, each playing a vital role in the movement of goods. Over the past two decades, international transport has experienced exponential growth, with surface and sea transportation witnessing a significant surge. Understanding the nuances of these transportation modes is essential for navigating the complexities of international trade effectively.

Join me as we embark on this journey through surface and sea transportation, unraveling the mechanisms that drive global commerce and trade. Let's delve into the heart of these vital transportation networks and uncover the keys to successful logistics in the modern era.

Topic 85: Ground transportation by road

When we delve into the realm of surface transportation, we encounter a mode of movement that is deeply rooted in history and continues to play a pivotal role in modern logistics. Ground transportation, often referred to as the oldest mode of transportation, traces its origins back to ancient times, with iconic routes like the Silk Road facilitating the exchange of goods across vast distances when sea transport was impractical.

Surface transportation, particularly road transportation, is renowned for its immediacy and flexibility, making it ideal for short-distance shipments and immediate needs. It serves as a crucial feeder to air and sea transportation, providing vital connectivity to these larger modes of transport.

However, road transportation also presents challenges. It can be costly, tiring, and environmentally polluting, with high variable costs associated, especially for truck movements. Despite these drawbacks, it remains the most common and practical mode of ground transportation.

In contrast, sea transportation reigns supreme in international trade, with affordability driving its dominance. Accounting for a staggering 90% of global goods movement between countries, sea transport boasts the capacity to carry vast quantities of cargo in a single voyage. Yet, it grapples with issues of pollution and environmental sustainability, posing significant challenges in today's context of heightened environmental awareness.

As we explore the intricacies of ground and sea transportation, we confront the dichotomy of their importance in global trade and their impact on the environment. Balancing the need for efficient logistics with environmental stewardship presents a formidable challenge as we navigate the complexities of modern transportation networks.

Topic 86: Sea transportation

Welcome to our voyage across the expansive oceans of international commerce. In this chapter, we embark on an exploration of sea transportation, a cornerstone of global trade and connectivity.

Sea transportation, epitomized by the movement of goods via ships across vast oceans and waterways, boasts several defining characteristics. Firstly, its unparalleled scale enables the transportation of immense quantities of cargo, making it indispensable for bulk shipments and large-scale trade. With sea routes linking major ports worldwide, sea transportation offers global reach on an unprecedented scale.

One of the key advancements in sea transportation is containerization, which has revolutionized cargo handling, enhancing efficiency, and reducing costs. Moreover, sea transport excels in ferrying goods across long distances, particularly between different countries and continents.

Despite its numerous advantages, sea transportation does present certain limitations. Ships are not the fastest mode of transport, posing challenges for time-sensitive cargo. Additionally, the infrastructure of ports and terminals must be adequately equipped to handle sea vessels, and accessibility can be problematic in certain regions.

Moreover, the transshipment requirement between sea and land-based transport can add complexity and time to the shipping process. Furthermore, sea transportation is susceptible to weather-related delays and piracy risks in certain regions, necessitating careful navigation and planning.

In conclusion, sea transportation offers a cost-effective and high-capacity solution for the long-distance transport of bulk and low-value goods. It provides global connectivity and environmental efficiency, albeit with challenges related to speed and infrastructure. As an essential component of international logistics, sea transportation serves as a vital conduit for connecting nations and facilitating global trade on a massive scale.

As we continue our exploration of transportation modes, we invite you to join us on our journey through the dynamic landscape of logistics. Stay tuned as we navigate through the intricacies of road, rail, and air transportation, unraveling the interconnected web of global commerce.

Topic 87: Transportation by trucks

In our exploration of transportation modes, let's steer our focus towards the backbone of ground logistics: transportation by trucks. As we delve into this segment, we'll uncover the diverse array of trucks and their pivotal role in the movement of goods.

Trucks, in various shapes and sizes, form the lifeline of ground transportation, facilitating the movement of goods across short and intermediate distances. From delivery vans to flatbed lorries, box bodies lorries to articulated lorries, the versatility of trucks is unmatched. These vehicles serve as the immediate and flexible solution for transporting goods, acting as vital feeders to sea transportation networks.

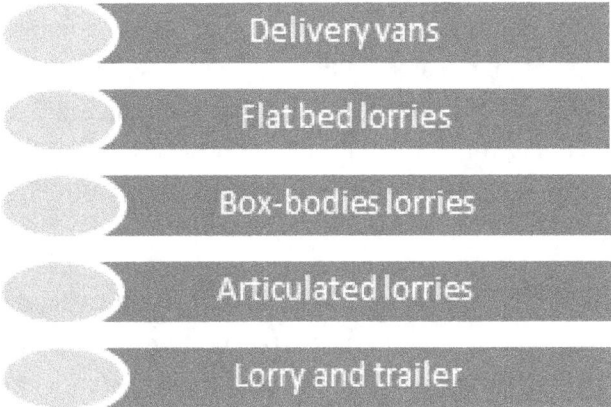

Delivery vans

Flat bed lorries

Box-bodies lorries

Articulated lorries

Lorry and trailer

However, it's essential to acknowledge the challenges that accompany truck transportation. High variable costs, while offering flexibility, present financial hurdles. Moreover, the environmental impact of truck emissions raises concerns about sustainability and pollution.

As we navigate through the complexities of international logistics, we must ponder solutions to mitigate these challenges. Striking a balance between efficiency and environmental responsibility is paramount. By fostering innovation and adopting sustainable practices, we can pave the way for a more eco-friendly and efficient transportation landscape.

So, let's embark on this journey with a keen eye towards sustainability and environmental stewardship, ensuring that our logistics practices align with the principles of responsible global trade.

Topic 88: Rail transportation

As we shift our focus to rail transportation, we enter the realm of efficient and specialized land logistics. Rail transportation, often overshadowed by its road counterpart, possesses unique characteristics and advantages that merit exploration.

Rail transportation excels in the movement of bulk products, offering a cost-effective solution for high tonnage shipments over long distances. While not as massive as ocean vessels, trains can transport substantial quantities of goods, with hundreds of cars capable of carrying several hundred metric tons of cargo. Moreover, rail transport can accommodate diverse product needs through specialized cars, such as tankers for liquids, refrigerated cars for perishables, and cars fitted with ramps for automobiles, reminiscent of the roll-on-roll-off (RoRo) ships in maritime transport.

The suitability of rail transportation extends to its efficiency and cost-effectiveness. In ideal conditions, rail transport proves less expensive than trucks and air transport, particularly for long-distance haulage. While challenges may arise in harsh conditions or remote areas, rail transportation boasts lower variable costs compared to road transport, with infrastructure and rolling stock forming the primary cost components.

In regions like the European Union, rail transport plays a significant role in intercontinental and domestic trade, underscoring its importance in global logistics networks. Despite its lesser spotlight, rail transportation remains a critical component of the transportation industry, offering reliability, efficiency, and cost advantages for the movement of goods across vast land distances.

Topic 89: Intermodal Transportation
Intermodal transportation stands at the crossroads of efficiency and innovation, revolutionizing the movement of goods across land routes. While it encompasses various modes of transportation, including sea and air, its significance shines brightest in the realm of land logistics.

At its core, intermodal transportation capitalizes on the standardization of containerization, unitization, and palletization, streamlining the mechanized handling of goods. This approach proves especially vital for intra-country and international land shipments, where containers reign supreme as the preferred method of cargo transport.

Dedicated freight corridors, such as those in India and China, exemplify the commitment to intermodal transportation, facilitating seamless cargo movement across vast land expanses. By harnessing the advantages of intermodal and multimodal transportation, businesses can mitigate risks associated with time loss, pilferage, and cargo damage, inherent in traditional cargo handling methods.

Moreover, intermodal transportation expedites cargo movement, simplifies documentation procedures, and reduces freight rates and insurance costs. Through collaboration with multimodal transport operators (MTOs), shippers gain a single point of contact for all aspects of cargo movement, including claims settlement, streamlining the logistics process.

Internationally, intermodal transportation offers exporters the flexibility to negotiate sales contracts based on delivered prices, simplifying cost calculations and enhancing market competitiveness. The through rates provided by MTOs empower exporters to navigate foreign markets with confidence, ensuring efficient and cost-effective delivery of goods to global buyers.

In essence, intermodal transportation epitomizes the synergy between innovation and logistics, ushering in an era of seamless cargo movement across land routes and beyond.

Topic 90: Common types of cargo in sea transportation

When delving into the realm of sea transportation, it's crucial to familiarize ourselves with the diverse types of cargo that navigate the vast oceans. Broadly speaking, sea cargo can be categorized into two main types: bulk cargo and break bulk/general cargo.

Bulk cargo encompasses primary commodities, both dry and liquid, that are typically transported in large quantities as shiploads. Examples include ores, fertilizers, food grains, crude oil, petroleum, and edible oils. These goods are often loaded directly into the ship's hold without individual packaging, facilitating efficient transport over long distances.

On the other hand, break bulk or general cargo refers to manufactured, semi-manufactured, processed, or semi-processed goods. These items are usually packaged in various forms such as wooden cases, crates, bales, drums, rolls, or bags. In shipping terminology, they are commonly referred to as general merchandise. This category covers a wide range of products, from electronics and machinery to textiles and consumer goods.

Understanding the different types of cargo is essential for grasping the nuances of interactions between carriers, shippers, and intermediaries. Each type of cargo demands unique handling and logistics considerations, influencing the choice of transportation methods and packaging solutions.

By discerning the intricacies of sea cargo classification, stakeholders can optimize supply chain operations, enhance efficiency, and ensure the seamless movement of goods across the maritime domain.

Topic 91: Types of Ocean Going Ships

In the expansive domain of sea transportation, it's imperative to acquaint ourselves with the various types of ocean-going ships that ply the world's oceans. These ships serve diverse purposes and are instrumental in facilitating the movement of goods across vast maritime routes.

First and foremost, we have bulkers, which are merchant ships designed to transport unpackaged bulk cargo such as grains, coal, cement, and ores in their cargo holds. These vessels are optimized for efficiently transporting large quantities of bulk commodities.

Next, container ships revolutionized the logistics industry by introducing standardized containers for cargo transport. These ships carry containers of varying sizes, with dimensions tailored to accommodate the efficient stacking and transport of these containers. Container ships range from Panamax vessels, which adhere to the maximum dimensions for passage through the Panama Canal, to ULCS (Ultra Large Container

Ships) capable of carrying thousands of TEUs (Twenty-foot Equivalent Units).

Specialty ships encompass a diverse range of vessel types tailored for specific cargo requirements. Tankers transport liquid cargoes such as crude oil, petroleum products, and chemicals, while Ro-Ro (Roll-on/Roll-off) ships facilitate the transport of wheeled cargo like automobiles and trailers. Additionally, we have livestock carriers, heavy lift vessels for transporting oversized or heavy cargo, and reefers equipped for transporting perishable goods under temperature-controlled conditions.

The evolution of container ships reflects the dynamic nature of maritime transport, with vessels continuously increasing in size and capacity to accommodate growing trade volumes and enhance efficiency. From early container ships carrying a few hundred TEUs to the emergence of Triple E vessels capable of transporting over 18,000 TEUs, the maritime industry continues to innovate to meet the demands of global commerce.

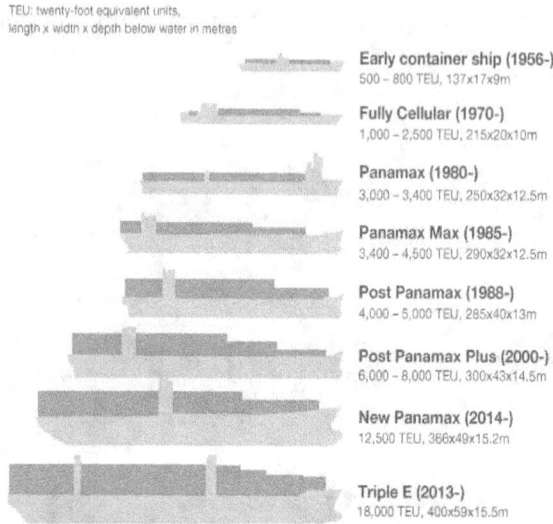

TEU: twenty-foot equivalent units,
length x width x depth below water in metres

Early container ship (1956-)
500 – 800 TEU, 137x17x9m

Fully Cellular (1970-)
1,000 – 2,500 TEU, 215x20x10m

Panamax (1980-)
3,000 – 3,400 TEU, 250x32x12.5m

Panamax Max (1985-)
3,400 – 4,500 TEU, 290x32x12.5m

Post Panamax (1988-)
4,000 – 5,000 TEU, 285x40x13m

Post Panamax Plus (2000-)
6,000 – 8,000 TEU, 300x43x14.5m

New Panamax (2014-)
12,500 TEU, 366x49x15.2m

Triple E (2013-)
18,000 TEU, 400x59x15.5m

By understanding the characteristics and capabilities of these different types of ocean-going ships, stakeholders in the shipping and logistics sectors can make informed decisions to optimize cargo transport, streamline operations, and drive efficiency in the global supply chain.

Topic 92: All About Chartering A Ship

As we delve deeper into the intricacies of sea transportation, it's essential to understand the pivotal role of chartering in facilitating the movement of goods across maritime routes. Chartering, an activity within the shipping industry, involves the hiring out of vessels by ship owners to charterers, who are typically shippers, through a contractual agreement known as a charter party.

In the realm of chartering, we encounter various types of arrangements tailored to meet diverse cargo requirements and operational needs. One such arrangement is liner services, where ships are designed to accommodate multiple cargo units, including containers from different shippers. These services operate on fixed voyages akin to scheduled flights, facilitating the movement of goods through transport documents such as bills of lading.

Conversely, chartering also encompasses arrangements for bulk cargoes through contracts known as charterparty agreements. Unlike liner services, chartering offers a greater degree of flexibility, with arrangements based on the principle of freedom of contract between ship owners and charterers. This flexibility allows for bespoke agreements tailored to specific cargo needs and voyage requirements.

Within the realm of chartering, we encounter various types of agreements, each serving distinct purposes and catering to different operational scenarios. Voyage charters involve the hiring of vessels for specific voyages between load and discharge ports, with payment based on factors such as tonnage or lump sum. Time charters, on the other hand, entail the hiring of vessels for a specified period, during which the charterer assumes operational control and covers expenses such as fuel and port charges.

Additionally, there are specialized arrangements such as bareboat charters, where the charterer assumes full control and financial responsibility for the vessel, including crewing and maintenance. Back-to-back charters involve a chain of charter parties between primary and sub-charterers, facilitating the seamless transfer of charter rights and obligations. Trip time charters, meanwhile, cater to short-term voyages on specified routes, offering flexibility for cargo such as vegetable oils or dry bulk.

In essence, chartering forms the backbone of sea transportation, offering a diverse range of agreements to meet the ever-evolving needs of global trade. By understanding the nuances of chartering, stakeholders can navigate the complexities of maritime logistics, optimize cargo transport, and drive efficiency in the global supply chain.

Topic 93: Contract of Afreightment

In the realm of maritime logistics, alongside chartering agreements, we encounter another crucial arrangement known as the Contract of Affreightment. This contract involves the ship owner undertaking to transport specified cargo within a designated timeframe and along a predetermined route. Unlike traditional charter parties, a Contract of Affreightment may involve the use of one or multiple ships, depending on the cargo volume and requirements.

Similar to charter parties, Contracts of Affreightment utilize bill of lading documents to formalize the transport agreement. However, the involvement of multiple ships or the possibility of less than one ship distinguishes it from traditional chartering arrangements. This flexibility makes Contracts of Affreightment particularly suitable for the movement of liquid and dry bulk cargo, where the exact shipping requirements may vary and are not always predetermined.

One notable aspect of Contracts of Affreightment is that the duration of the chartering period is directly related to the total quantity of cargo to be transported. This means that the charterer is primarily concerned with ensuring the movement of a specific volume of cargo, rather than the number of ships involved. As a result, the risk of delays in fulfilling the contract typically falls on the ship owner, who is responsible for ensuring the timely delivery of the cargo.

In terms of freight calculations, Contracts of Affreightment typically operate on a tonnage basis rather than a lump sum payment. This means that the freight charges are directly proportional to the weight of the cargo being transported, offering a transparent and straightforward pricing structure for both parties involved.

Overall, Contracts of Affreightment serve as a flexible and efficient means of transporting bulk quantities of cargo, particularly in industries where shipment volumes may fluctuate or where precise shipping requirements are not always known in advance. With its focus on cargo quantity and tonnage-based freight calculations, this arrangement provides a practical solution for shippers seeking reliable and cost-effective maritime transport solutions.

Topic 94: Vessel Flags and Flag Conferences

In the intricate world of maritime trade, understanding vessel flags and flag conferences is essential to grasp the dynamics of sea transportation. Vessel flags symbolize the country in which a ship is registered, known as the ship registry. However, ship owners sometimes opt for a "flag of convenience," enabling them to register their ships under foreign flags for practical reasons. This flexibility allows them to adapt to changing geopolitical situations and operational needs, mitigating capital costs associated with sticking to a single national flag.

Moreover, shipping conferences play a crucial role in managing routes, capacity, tonnage, and freight charges within the maritime industry. These conferences often involve associations or cartels comprising multiple shipping lines collaborating to streamline operations and optimize resources. Similarly, flag conferences bring together multiple flags, facilitating cooperative arrangements among various maritime jurisdictions.

Such activities and associations are indispensable for the smooth functioning of sea transportation. Without them, coordinating routes, managing capacity, and setting freight charges would be significantly more challenging, making efficient maritime trade operations difficult to achieve. Thus, vessel flags and flag conferences serve as vital components of the maritime trade ecosystem, enabling seamless navigation of international waters and facilitating global commerce.

Topic 95: NVOCCs and Section Take Away

Non-vessel operating common carriers (NVOCCs) play a distinct role in the realm of sea transportation. Unlike vessel operating common carriers (VOCCs) such as Maersk or APL, NVOCCs do not own vessels. However, they function similarly to carriers and provide services akin to freight forwarders. NVOCCs are particularly well-suited for small and medium-sized international traders who may not have the capacity or resources to engage directly with large carriers. These traders rely on NVOCCs for their expertise and flexibility in handling smaller-scale shipments without the need for extensive contracts.

In this section, we have delved into various aspects of sea and surface transportation, exploring the nature of equipment, methods, capabilities, costs, and different types of arrangements and service providers. Understanding these intricacies is crucial for gaining a comprehensive understanding of sea transportation and its associated processes.

As we conclude this section, I trust you have found it informative and enlightening. If there are any additional aspects you believe should be included or further explored, please feel free to share your thoughts via private messaging. Your feedback is invaluable as we strive to enhance the comprehensiveness of this book.

Thank you for your engagement and participation.

Topic 96: Ocean Freight Rates And Factors Influencing These Rates

Ocean freight rates are pivotal in the realm of sea transportation, dictating the cost of shipping goods across vast distances. At its core, an ocean freight rate denotes the base rate for transporting goods on a particular voyage for a specific commodity. However, the nuances of ocean freight rates extend beyond this simplistic definition.

Containerization, a revolutionary advancement in sea transportation, has ushered in a new era of efficiency and scalability. Within containerization, two primary types of rates prevail: LCL (Less than Container Load) and FCL (Full Container Load) rates.

LCL rates apply when the cargo being transported does not fill an entire container. In such cases, the cost is calculated based on either the weight in tons or the volume in cubic meters of the shipment, whichever is higher. This figure is then multiplied by the base rate set by the shipping line.

On the other hand, FCL rates come into play when the cargo fills an entire container. The base rate for FCL shipments is determined by the container's capacity, whether it's a 20ft or 40ft container. Typically, FCL rates come with substantial discounts compared to LCL rates, owing to the efficiency of filling entire containers. These discounts are often negotiated as part of the arrangement with the shipping line.

In summary, while LCL rates may be higher on a per-unit basis compared to FCL rates, the latter offers cost advantages due to the utilization of entire containers. Understanding these distinctions is crucial for businesses engaged in international trade, as it enables informed decision-making regarding the most cost-effective shipping methods for their goods.

Understanding the factors that influence ocean freight rates is crucial for businesses engaged in international trade. While the base rate serves as a starting point, numerous dynamics come into play, shaping the final cost of shipping goods across oceans.

Liner rates, for instance, represent standard shipping line tariffs, with discounts often available for frequent shippers or established freight forwarders. In contrast, charter rates fluctuate based on demand and supply, reflecting the negotiation prowess of stakeholders and the specific nature of the cargo.

Moreover, different rates apply to specific types of goods, with considerations for congestion charges at busy ports and currency adjustment factors to account for exchange rate fluctuations. The bunker adjustment factor accommodates fuel price variations, while surcharges, such as security surcharges, cover regulatory costs or specific port requirements.

Seasonality also plays a role, with high-demand periods driving up prices, while country currency and terminal fees further impact the final freight rates. Fines, fees, and terminal capacities contribute to the complexity of rate determination, emphasizing the need for a comprehensive understanding of the myriad factors at play in the ocean freight market.

In conclusion, navigating ocean freight rates requires a nuanced understanding of the interplay between these multifaceted factors, enabling businesses to optimize their shipping strategies and mitigate costs effectively.

Topic 97: Common Shipping/Customs Formalities

When it comes to shipping and customs formalities, there are several key steps that exporters need to navigate to ensure smooth transportation of goods across borders.

Firstly, exporters must prepare and submit the necessary export documents, including the shipping bill, which serves as the export declaration. This submission initiates the customs process, allowing authorities to verify the documents and assign a shipping bill number.

Next, customs officials in the origin country assess the value of the goods before issuing a carting order, which authorizes the movement of the cargo within the port premises. This step, often overseen by port trust authorities, ensures compliance with customs regulations and port procedures.

Following this, customs examination may be conducted to verify the contents of the shipment, leading to the issuance of a Let Export order by the customs examiner. Additionally, a Let Ship order may be obtained from the customs preventive officer, further facilitating the export process.

Once the goods are loaded onto the vessel, the captain issues a Mate's Receipt (MR), confirming receipt of the cargo on board. With the necessary clearances from customs and port authorities, the shipper can then obtain the bill of lading from the carrier, finalizing the shipping documentation and enabling the goods to commence their journey to the destination.

Topic 98: Common intermediaries in Sea Transport Management

In sea transportation, various intermediaries play crucial roles in facilitating the movement of goods and ensuring smooth operations across borders. Let's delve into some of these common intermediaries and their functions:

Customs Brokers: These individuals are licensed by local customs authorities to handle all documentation and procedures involved in customs clearance for both export and import cargo. They serve as customs experts, navigating the complex regulations and requirements.

Freight Forwarders (NVOCCs): Also known as Non-Vessel Operating Common Carriers (NVOCCs), freight forwarders provide comprehensive support for the transportation of goods. They serve as logistics experts, arranging the transportation, warehousing, and distribution of goods across various modes of transport, including sea freight.

Shipping Agents: Acting as representatives of ship owners, shipping agents coordinate all matters related to ships' operations. They liaise with port authorities, handle documentation, and oversee logistical arrangements for vessels, serving as experts in ship management.

Stevedores: Commonly referred to as dockers or dockworkers, stevedores are manual labor supervisors stationed at waterfront ports. Their primary role involves the loading and unloading of cargo onto and from ships at port facilities. They possess expertise in handling cargo efficiently and safely in maritime environments.

These intermediaries play integral roles in the sea transport management ecosystem, each contributing specialized knowledge and services to ensure the seamless movement of goods through international trade routes.

Topic 99: Important sea routes and international sea ports

In sea transportation, understanding important sea routes and international sea ports is crucial for efficient global trade. Let's explore some of these vital routes and ports:

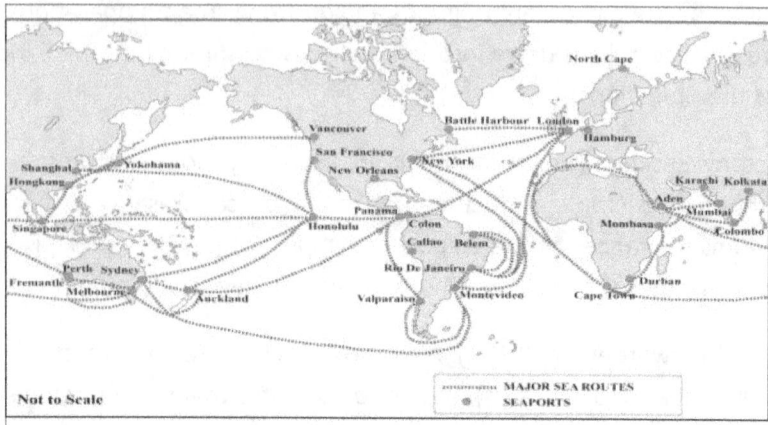

English Channel: Serving as a key waterway between the UK and mainland Europe, the English Channel is a critical route for trade and transportation.

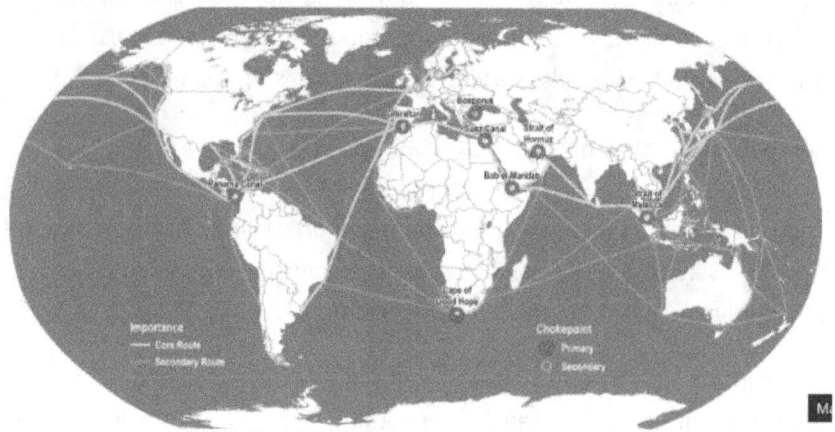

Straits of Malacca: Located between the Malay Peninsula and the Indonesian island of Sumatra, the Straits of Malacca is one of the busiest and most strategic waterways, facilitating trade between the Indian Ocean and the Pacific Ocean.

Panama Canal: This man-made canal in Central America connects the Atlantic and Pacific Oceans, significantly reducing travel time and costs for ships transiting between the two oceans.

Suez Canal: Another crucial man-made waterway, the Suez Canal in Egypt provides a shortcut between the Mediterranean Sea and the Red Sea, facilitating trade between Europe and Asia.

South and East China Seas: These maritime regions are vital for trade, serving as major routes for shipping between Asia, Oceania, and beyond.

Straits of Hormuz: Located between the Persian Gulf and the Gulf of Oman, the Straits of Hormuz is a critical chokepoint for oil transportation, with significant geopolitical implications.

Straits of Gibraltar: Connecting the Atlantic Ocean to the Mediterranean Sea, the Straits of Gibraltar is a strategic passage for trade between Europe and Africa.

Danish Straits: Comprising the Øresund, Great Belt, and Little Belt, the Danish Straits are essential waterways for maritime traffic in the Baltic Sea region.

Saint Lawrence Seaway: Connecting the Great Lakes to the Atlantic Ocean, the Saint Lawrence Seaway is a vital trade route for North America.

These sea routes are supported by numerous international sea ports, acting as crucial endpoints for maritime trade. Major ports like Shanghai, Hong Kong, Singapore, Rotterdam, New York, and Dubai facilitate the movement of goods and serve as hubs for global commerce. Understanding these sea routes and ports is essential for navigating the complexities of international trade and transportation.

In conclusion, this chapter has provided a comprehensive overview of surface and sea transportation, covering various concepts, arrangements, intermediaries, and key factors influencing freight rates. We delved into topics such as contracts of affreightment, vessel flags and conferences, NVOCCs, ocean freight rates, shipping/customs formalities, and important sea routes and ports.

Throughout the chapter, we explored the intricate network of global trade routes, the roles of different stakeholders, and the significance of strategic chokepoints. From understanding the dynamics of freight negotiations to navigating the complexities of customs clearance, each aspect plays a crucial role in ensuring the smooth flow of goods across borders and oceans.

By grasping the fundamentals of sea transportation, including the roles of intermediaries, the intricacies of freight rates, and the importance of sea routes and ports, we gain a deeper insight into the world of international trade and logistics. This knowledge equips us with the tools to make informed decisions, optimize supply chain operations, and adapt to the ever-changing landscape of global commerce.

As we conclude this chapter, it is evident that a strong understanding of surface and sea transportation is essential for businesses involved in international trade. By continuously learning and adapting to new developments in the industry, we can navigate the challenges and seize the opportunities that arise in the dynamic world of logistics and transportation.

Chapter 13: Dry Ports

Topic 100: Chapter Overview

Welcome to the next chapter on dry ports. In this section, we will delve into the pivotal role of dry ports in facilitating the movement of goods on an international scale and optimizing logistics costs.

Dry ports, also known as inland ports, serve as essential hubs in the transportation network, connecting land-based transportation modes with maritime shipping. Throughout this chapter, we will explore the significance of dry ports, their functions, and the facilities they offer. Additionally, we will examine the challenges faced by dry ports and the factors that drive their development and success.

As we progress, we will gain a deeper understanding of how dry ports contribute to enhancing the efficiency and effectiveness of supply chain operations. We will also analyze a case study focusing on the dry port scenario in India, shedding light on the impact of a robust dry port network on the economy and logistics landscape of a nation.

By the end of this section, you will have a comprehensive understanding of the vital role played by dry ports in international logistics management. So let's embark on this journey to uncover the significance of dry ports and their implications for global trade and commerce. Thank you for joining me on this exploration. Let's dive into the world of dry ports.

Topic 101: Dry Ports – An Introduction

Introducing dry ports - an essential component of the global logistics network. Dry ports, unlike traditional seaports, are inland terminals located in the hinterland, away from the coastlines. These strategic hubs play a crucial role in facilitating the handling and temporary storage of containers, both for general and bulk cargoes.

Primarily serving containers, dry ports have become indispensable due to the advent of containerization, revolutionizing international and domestic logistics. They offer a range of services, including full customs clearance and border control, making them key players in facilitating smooth trade operations.

Dry ports come in various forms, with two main categories being Inland Container Depots (ICDs) and Container Freight Stations (CFS). ICDs provide comprehensive services, including customs-related functions, while CFS mainly focus on temporary storage and consolidation of containers.

Whether located near seaports or in the hinterland, dry ports serve as vital nodes in the supply chain, ensuring efficient movement of goods between different modes of transportation. Join us as we delve deeper into the role and significance of dry ports in optimizing logistics operations.

Topic 102: Why do we need dry ports in addition to sea ports?

Why do we need dry ports in addition to sea ports? The answer lies in addressing several key factors that shape the global logistics landscape. Firstly, for landlocked countries or regions without adequate port infrastructure, dry ports serve as crucial gateways to international trade. Even in maritime nations like India or Brazil, existing sea ports often face limitations in capacity and accessibility, particularly for industries located in the hinterland.

Dry ports offer a solution by providing storage, customs clearance, and other essential services closer to industrial areas, reducing the need for costly and inconvenient long-distance transportation to sea ports. Moreover, as sea ports and airports become increasingly congested due to limited space and growing demand, dry ports play a vital role in expanding capacity and managing congestion effectively.

Furthermore, in large countries with extensive hinterlands like Russia or China, dry ports facilitate seamless access to global markets by integrating with nationwide supply chains. By acting as hubs for containerized cargo and streamlining logistics operations, dry ports contribute to reducing overall transportation costs and enhancing efficiency in the supply chain.

In essence, the establishment of dry ports complements sea ports by providing a network of inland terminals that enhance connectivity, alleviate congestion, and optimize logistics processes, thereby playing a pivotal role in facilitating international trade and economic growth.

Topic 103: What are typical facilities made available at dry ports?

What are the typical facilities made available at dry ports? Dry ports are equipped with a range of facilities to support efficient handling, storage, and transportation of goods. Firstly, intermodal transport and handling of goods are key activities at dry ports, facilitating the smooth movement of international-bound cargo.

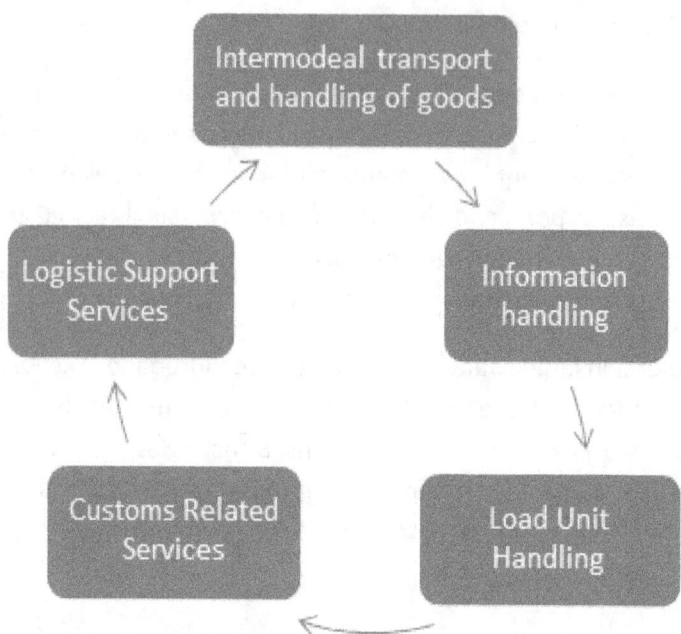

In addition, modern information handling infrastructure plays a crucial role in optimizing supply chain processes. Dry ports are equipped with robust information systems, including IT-enabled and even artificial intelligence-enabled platforms, to manage data effectively and enhance logistical efficiency.

Load unit handling services and facilities are another essential feature of dry ports. These facilities include equipment for handling containers of various sizes and weights, enabling efficient stowing, storage, stacking, loading, and unloading of cargo. Dry ports often boast state-of-the-art handling equipment comparable to those found at seaports.

Furthermore, dry ports provide comprehensive customs-related services, ensuring seamless border control and customs clearance processes. These facilities are equipped with modern infrastructure and the latest equipment to support customs authorities in their duties, often surpassing the capabilities of seaports in this regard.

Logistics support services and infrastructure are also essential components of dry ports. These include facilities for truck and train gating, warehousing, consolidation, and container yards. Rail sliding facilities are particularly important for rail-based terminals, which are prevalent in countries like India with dedicated freight corridors.

Moreover, dry ports feature warehouses of varying sizes to accommodate cargo storage requirements, ranging from smaller warehouses for Inland Container Depots (ICDs) to larger warehouses for Container Freight Stations (CFS). Additionally, modern gate complexes equipped with advanced equipment and information systems ensure smooth ingress and egress of cargo, facilitating efficient customs clearance processes.

In summary, dry ports are equipped with a comprehensive array of facilities and infrastructure to support the seamless flow of goods, optimize logistical processes, and enhance trade efficiency.

Topic 104: About customs clearance at dry ports

About customs clearance at dry ports: Dry ports play a pivotal role in facilitating customs clearance for both export and import activities. Specifically, Inland Container Depots (ICDs) serve as crucial hubs for customs formalities, enabling seamless shipment processing without the need to transport cargo to seaports.

At ICDs, exporters can complete all necessary customs procedures, including border control formalities, before the cargo reaches seaports. This eliminates the need for additional time and effort associated with customs clearance at seaports, streamlining the export process.

In situations where overseas buyers require an on board bill of lading as proof of export, exporters may need to wait until the cargo reaches the seaport. During this interim period, exporters can obtain a Received for Shipment Bill of Lading from the carrier, serving as proof of shipment and customs clearance at the dry port.

One distinctive feature of dry ports is the provision of on-premises customs clearance facilities, particularly for full container load shipments. This facility, available for both 20-foot and 40-foot containers, is advantageous due to the dry port's accessibility to industrial areas in the hinterland. On-premises customs clearance streamlines the process, enhancing efficiency and reducing transit times.

The concept of on-premises customs clearance underscores the importance of dry ports, particularly Inland Container Depots, in facilitating international trade and optimizing logistical processes.

Topic 105: *Most essential requirements for running ICDs/CFSs*

Most essential requirements for running ICDs/CFSs: Running an Inland Container Depot (ICD) or a Container Freight Station (CFS) demands certain fundamental prerequisites to ensure seamless operations and efficient services for exporters and importers.

First and foremost, these facilities must function as common user facilities, accessible to all types of traders, exporters, and importers. They should be endowed with public authority status, equipped with fixed installations, and offer comprehensive services for handling and temporary storage of both import and export goods, including empty containers under customs control and supervision.

Ensuring the integrity of cargo is paramount, especially in hinterland locations where customs clearance occurs. Therefore, robust security measures, including proper sealing of containers, are imperative to prevent tampering and fraud before goods reach seaports.

Furthermore, customs and other relevant agencies operating within these facilities should possess the necessary personnel, equipment, and expertise to clear goods for various purposes, such as exports, warehousing, temporary admission, re-export, onward transit, and outright export. They should be well-versed in the diverse requirements of facility users and facilitate the transshipment of cargo effectively.

For Container Freight Stations, additional fixed installations such as warehouses may be necessary to accommodate the storage and handling of cargo. Overall, adherence to these essential requirements ensures the smooth functioning and reliability of ICDs/CFSs, facilitating international trade and logistics seamlessly.

Topic 106: Dry port echosystem and growth of dry port infrastructure in India- A Case Study

Examining the landscape of dry ports in countries like India offers insights into how these facilities facilitate the movement of goods across vast territories, even from remote areas, fostering a comprehensive international logistics system. In India, the development of dry ports gained significant attention with the establishment of the Inter-Ministerial Committee (IMC) in 1992, chaired by the Additional Secretary of Infrastructure, Ministry of Commerce. This committee was tasked with overseeing the development of dry ports, recognizing their pivotal role in a country as expansive as India.

Since the inception of this initiative in 1989, India has witnessed remarkable progress, boasting a network of approximately 283 dry ports, encompassing both Inland Container Depots (ICDs) and Container Freight Stations (CFSs). While CFSs are strategically located near seaports to provide essential services like warehousing and congestion management, ICDs, numbering 147, offer comprehensive services, including customs facilities, catering to inland regions.

However, with many ICDs experiencing congestion and land constraints, warehousing and consolidation services are often facilitated through CFSs. Of the total dry ports in India, around 40% are owned by government departments or public sector units associated with the Indian government, with the majority being part of multi-modal transport operations. The remaining dry ports are privately owned, although government agencies predominantly oversee their planning and integration into the national logistics system.

This case study sheds light on India's proactive approach to dry port development, illustrating how government-led initiatives have propelled the growth of essential infrastructure vital for facilitating trade and enhancing logistical efficiencies on a national scale.

Examining the drivers and challenges within India's dry port sector provides valuable insights into its evolution and ongoing dynamics. The growth of Inland Container Depots (ICDs) in India is primarily propelled by the exponential increase in port traffic following the liberalization and globalization initiatives of the early 1990s. This surge in port activities necessitated the establishment of dry ports to cater to the burgeoning demand for customs clearance services, particularly at ICDs where such activities have seen substantial growth.

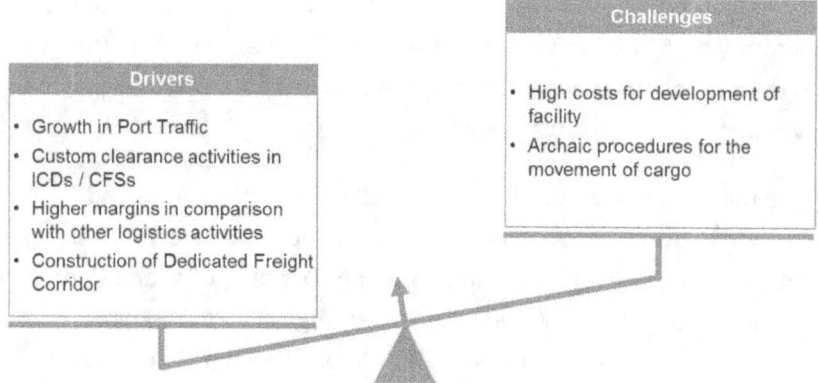

Private entities operating these dry ports find them lucrative, yielding higher margins compared to other logistics activities within the country. Additionally, the construction of dedicated freight corridors in India has further boosted the relevance and significance of dry ports, enhancing their role in the national logistics landscape.

However, amidst the growth, several challenges persist. The high capital costs associated with developing dry port facilities pose a significant barrier to entry, limiting the involvement of smaller players. Moreover, India's complex and archaic cargo movement procedures, coupled with challenges related to land acquisition, environmental clearances, and rehabilitation costs, hinder the smooth development of dry ports. Lengthy processes for land acquisition and railway clearances, compounded by the poor performance of some contractors, further exacerbate the challenges faced by stakeholders in the dry port ecosystem.

Despite these hurdles, ongoing efforts to streamline procedures, improve infrastructure, and address environmental concerns underscore India's commitment to fostering the growth of its dry port infrastructure. By addressing these challenges proactively, India aims to bolster its position as a key player in the global logistics arena.

Topic 107: Section Take Away

In conclusion, our exploration of dry ports, particularly within the context of India, has shed light on the critical role they play in global logistics management. As showcased in the case study, the challenges and growth drivers experienced in India are reflective of those encountered in many large countries worldwide.

The establishment and growth of dry ports are driven by factors such as the surge in port traffic, increased demand for customs clearance services, and the attractiveness of higher margins for private operators. However, challenges such as high capital costs, complex regulatory procedures, and logistical hurdles underscore the need for concerted efforts and government support to overcome them.

It's evident that the success of dry ports hinges on collaboration between public and private entities, with local governments playing a pivotal role in facilitating their planning and implementation. The significance of dry ports in facilitating international trade and optimizing logistics costs cannot be overstated, particularly in the era of containerization, where they serve as crucial nodes in the supply chain network.

As you delve deeper into the world of dry ports, I encourage you to explore the provided external resources for a comprehensive understanding of their intricacies, particularly in the Indian context. By leveraging this knowledge, you'll be well-equipped to appreciate the significance of dry ports in the broader logistics landscape and recognize their indispensable role in supporting global trade.

Chapter 15: Export by Air

Topic 109: Chapter Overview

Welcome to this section where we'll explore the intricacies of exporting goods by air. Whether you're a seasoned logistics professional or new to the field, understanding the nuances of air freight, customs procedures, and documentation is essential for navigating the global trade landscape efficiently.

Throughout this section, we'll delve into the fundamental concepts of exporting by air, covering everything from the basics of air freight to the intricacies of customs clearance procedures at airports worldwide. My aim is to provide you with a comprehensive overview of the steps involved in exporting by air, along with practical insights and answers to frequently asked questions.

While each country may have its own specific requirements and regulations, the core principles and logic behind the export process remain consistent. By familiarizing yourself with these principles, you'll be better equipped to navigate the complexities of air cargo logistics and ensure smooth and efficient exports.

So, let's embark on this journey together as we explore the evolution of air cargo movement, understand the key concepts, and unravel the intricacies of exporting goods by air. Let's dive in and uncover the essentials of air exports.

Thank you for joining me, and let's get started!

Topic 110: A brief history of movement of cargo by air

The story of air cargo transportation traces back to humble yet pivotal beginnings, rooted in the need for swift mail delivery. In its nascent stages, air cargo primarily served the purpose of expediting mail delivery, with a focus on transporting mail between regions, both within and outside countries.

One of the earliest recorded instances of air cargo usage dates back to the British rule in India, specifically in the United Province of Agra and Oudh. This inaugural use of air cargo was centered around postal services, highlighting the early emphasis on swiftly transporting mail across various regions.

As the 20th century progressed, air cargo evolved beyond mail delivery to become a vital component of global trade and commerce. Initially handling essential items like medicines and daily necessities, air cargo soon expanded its spectrum to include the transportation of heavy machinery parts and even film prints across Europe.

The innovative approach of using air cargo for transporting film prints ensured timely availability of cinematic content to theaters across Europe, showcasing the adaptability and significance of air cargo in meeting diverse logistical needs.

The late 20th century marked a transformative period for air cargo, with the emergence of affordable cargo airlines and technological advancements in aero technology. These developments led to the transportation of a wide range of goods across continents, revolutionizing international trade and commerce.

With advancements in tracking systems, air cargo became more transparent and accessible, attracting international traders to venture into untapped markets with confidence. Today, air cargo continues to play a fundamental role in global trade, accommodating a vast array of goods and ensuring timely delivery worldwide.

In an increasingly interconnected world, air cargo remains indispensable, contributing significantly to the seamless movement of commodities and the interconnectedness of nations and economies across the globe.

Topic 111: How does export by air work?

Exporting goods by air involves a structured process designed to ensure efficient and timely transportation of cargo worldwide. Understanding this process entails breaking it down into seven main steps, each crucial for the cargo's journey from its origin to its destination.

The first step is registration or pickup of the cargo, where the process begins by determining the chargeable weight of the shipment. This weight calculation is essential for determining shipping costs. Once this is done, a reliable shipping partner is selected, and the cargo is picked up by the airline and securely stored in the shipping company's warehouse before being loaded onto the aircraft.

Next is the step of confirmation and labeling. Upon receipt, the cargo undergoes rigorous quality checks to ensure its physical condition. It is then meticulously labeled with comprehensive details, adhering to international standards for labeling. Additionally, an air waybill is prepared, containing essential information for the cargo's onward journey by air.

The third step involves customs clearance at the airport of origin. Before departure, the cargo undergoes stringent scrutiny by the customs department at the airport of origin. This process ensures compliance with regulations and verifies that the consignment does not contain any prohibited or dangerous items.

Stay tuned for the subsequent steps in the export by air process to understand its full scope and intricacies.

Step four in the export by air process involves storage and departure. Once customs clearance is obtained at the origin airport, the cargo is packed into unit load devices (ULDs), which are specialized containers tailored for air transportation. These ULDs are then loaded onto the aircraft for transit to the destination.

Upon reaching the destination airport, the cargo is efficiently unloaded from the aircraft in step five. Accompanied by the air waybill created before departure, the cargo undergoes another round of customs clearance at the destination airport in step six. Once compliance is confirmed, the consignment is authorized for entry into the destination country.

The seventh and final step is delivery. After customs clearance at the destination airport, the cargo is transferred into containers for onward transportation to its final destination, whether it be a warehouse or another location. This last leg of the journey typically involves road, railway, or inland waterway transportation to ensure the goods reach their intended endpoint.

Each step in the airfreight process is meticulously orchestrated to ensure the secure and timely movement of goods across borders worldwide. The seamless coordination between shipping companies, customs authorities, and transportation networks is crucial for the smooth execution of air cargo operations.

The dynamism and efficiency of air freight have made it an indispensable component of global trade. Its ability to swiftly transport a diverse range of goods across vast distances fosters international commerce and enables businesses to access distant markets efficiently.

In conclusion, the streamlined process of air cargo movement exemplifies the precision and efficiency required to navigate the complexities of global logistics. By facilitating the movement of goods, air freight drives economic growth on a global scale.

Topic 112: Air way bill

Before delving deeper into the intricacies of exporting by air, it's crucial to understand the cornerstone document that facilitates this process: the air waybill.

The air waybill, often referred to as the AWB, serves as the primary transport document for goods transported via air cargo. Similar to the bill of lading used in sea freight, the air waybill acts as a binding contract between the shipper and the carrier, laying out the terms and conditions of transportation.

Comprising multiple copies, one of which accompanies the shipment throughout its journey, the air waybill plays a pivotal role in ensuring transparency and facilitating smooth transactions among all parties involved in the shipment.

One of the key components of the air waybill is the detailed information regarding the shipper and the consignee. The shipper, responsible for sending the goods, and the consignee, the intended recipient, must have their names and addresses meticulously outlined in the air waybill. This ensures clarity and accuracy in the shipment process, facilitating seamless communication between all parties involved.

Another crucial component of the air waybill is the inclusion of origin and destination airport codes. These codes, assigned to every airport worldwide, provide clarity regarding the actual origins and destinations of the cargo. By specifying these codes in the air waybill, clear guidance is provided on the routing of the cargo, ensuring efficient transportation.

Furthermore, a detailed description of the cargo is essential in the air waybill, akin to the bill of lading used in sea freight. This comprehensive description aids in the handling and categorization of goods throughout the transportation process, facilitating smooth operations.

Additionally, any special instructions pertinent to the handling of the cargo are explicitly stated within the air waybill. These instructions ensure adherence to unique conditions or protocols during transit, as mandated by the contract of international sale.

One of the distinctive features of the air waybill is its legal enforceability. Unlike the bill of lading, it is not a negotiable instrument. However, its legality empowers it to serve as a binding contract, facilitating the resolution of disputes or discrepancies that may arise during transportation. This legal significance provides clarity, accountability, and a basis for resolution, safeguarding the interests of both the shipper and the carrier.

In conclusion, the air waybill stands as a cornerstone in air cargo, encapsulating crucial details and serving as a testament to the agreement between the shipper and the carrier. Its meticulous documentation and legal significance underscore its pivotal role in ensuring the integrity and efficiency of global air freight operations.

Topic 113: Air freight costing, pricing and classification of air cargo

In the realm of international trading, understanding the intricacies of air freight costing and pricing is paramount. Air freight, while being the fastest mode of transportation, also commands higher prices compared to road or sea transportation. The rates of air freight can range significantly higher, approximately 4 to 5 times more than road transportation and up to 12 to 16 times more than sea routes.

Typically falling within the bracket of $1.5 to $4.5 per kilogram, air freight rates are subject to various determinants that shape the pricing structure. Let's delve into these determinants, the key factors influencing air freight costs and pricing:

Fuel Prices: Fluctuations in global fuel prices have a significant impact on air freight rates. The aviation industry's heavy reliance on aviation fuel makes fuel costs a major component of air freight expenses.

Shipment Type: The type of shipment greatly influences air freight costs. Standard shipments generally incur lower charges, while goods requiring specific climatic conditions or specialized handling typically result in higher expenses due to added service requirements.

Another critical factor in air freight costing and pricing is the space and chargeable weight of the cargo. Freight charges are influenced by the space occupied by the shipment within a Unit Load Device (ULD), which is equivalent to a container in sea shipment. Shipments occupying less than a full ULD load may incur costs proportional to the space they occupy and their weight, with discounts generally unavailable.

Distance and route are also significant determinants of air freight cost. The distance between origin and destination airports significantly impacts air freight costs, with longer distances typically resulting in higher expenses. However, certain air cargo routes, despite being longer, may offer more affordable rates due to high international trading volumes, ensuring consistent business flow for carriers.

In conclusion, while air freight remains the priciest option, its unparalleled speed and reliability make it indispensable for time-sensitive and perishable goods. Understanding the factors influencing air freight cost and pricing is crucial for international businesses navigating the logistics landscape. Balancing speed and cost-effectiveness remains a strategic consideration for shippers seeking optimal transportation solutions in a globally interconnected world market.

Now, let's explore freight calculations, a fundamental aspect of air cargo logistics. Calculating air freight involves understanding various weight metrics, including gross weight, volumetric weight, and chargeable weight, which significantly impact shipping costs.

Gross weight encompasses the total weight of the goods, including packaging and pallet weights. For example, if a product weighs 50kg and additional packaging and pallet weight totals 20kg, the gross weight would be 70kg.

Airlines also consider volumetric weight, especially for bulky but lightweight packages with less density. Volumetric weight is calculated by multiplying the package's volume by the applicable dimensional factor, ensuring efficient use of limited space in aircraft.

Another crucial aspect of air freight calculations is the dimensional factor, decided by airlines and typically varying around 167kg/m³. For instance, if a cargo with a gross weight of 70kg has dimensions of 2m width, 1.5m length, and 1m height, the volumetric weight would be calculated as 3 cubic meters multiplied by the dimensional factor (167kg/m³), resulting in 501kg. This volumetric weight, significantly higher than the gross weight, becomes the chargeable weight, determining the shipping cost.

Additionally, the classification of air cargo into general and special containers plays a vital role in pricing. General containers accommodate a wide range of products that do not require specialized storage conditions, making them cost-effective. These containers cater to items like clothes, electronics, pharmaceuticals, and more, with pricing based on standard weight metrics.

On the other hand, special containers are equipped with advanced features to cater to sensitive cargo, such as perishable goods, livestock, or fragile items. These containers have sophisticated systems like temperature and moisture control mechanisms to maintain optimal conditions, mitigating risks during transportation. Special containers are crucial for items requiring precise environmental control to prevent damage or spoilage, ensuring the integrity of the cargo throughout the journey.

Topic 114: Key document required

In the realm of export by air, several key documents play crucial roles in facilitating smooth transactions and ensuring compliance with regulations. One such document is the air waybill, which serves as the primary transport document, binding the shipper and the carrier in a contractual agreement for the shipment's journey via air cargo.

Additionally, documents like the commercial invoice, packing list, certificate of origin, and insurance certificate are commonly utilized in air exports. While these documents remain similar to those used in sea transportation, certain modifications are made to accommodate the specifics of air transport, such as mentioning the airport as the port of loading.

Moreover, for shipments containing hazardous or dangerous goods, the Dangerous Goods Declaration, mandated by IATA, is essential. This document ensures that proper precautions are taken in handling and packing such goods to prevent any potential risks during transportation. We have delved into the details of this declaration in previous sections of this book.

Another essential document in the realm of export by air is the Shipper's Letter of Instructions (SLI). Similar to its counterpart in sea transportation, the SLI for air transport is crucial for providing instructions to the freight forwarder or clearing and forwarding agent specialized in air transportation. This document ensures smooth coordination with airlines, efficient handling of cargo, and adherence to air transport regulations.

Additionally, the Destination Control Statement holds significance, especially in air exports due to the sensitivity of certain goods. While applicable to both air and sea exports, this statement is commonly associated with air shipments, outlining specific restrictions or controls regarding the destination of the goods.

Furthermore, documents like the fumigation certificate or phytosanitary certificate may be required for certain shipments, as mandated by the overseas buyer or local authorities. These certificates ensure compliance with regulations related to pest control and sanitation, safeguarding the integrity of the goods during international transit.

The Destination Control Statement is a crucial declaration made by the exporter, typically included in the commercial invoice or other relevant documents within the export documentation set. This statement is mandated for specific goods and serves to confirm the intended destination and end use of the exported products.

Essentially, the Destination Control Statement signifies that the goods are intended for use solely in the designated end-use country and not for purposes that could compromise security or violate export regulations. It acts as a safeguard against the diversion of goods to unauthorized destinations or for unauthorized purposes.

This statement is typically required by the export administration of the origin country and aims to maintain control over the movement and use of sensitive goods. It helps prevent the misuse of products, unauthorized redistribution, or potential risks associated with the unauthorized transfer of technology or sensitive materials.

While the formalities for the Destination Control Statement may vary from country to country, its underlying purpose remains consistent across jurisdictions. It is part of the broader export control regime, ensuring compliance with regulations governing the export of sensitive items and often requiring additional licenses or permissions for their export.

Ultimately, the Destination Control Statement plays a vital role in maintaining oversight and control over the export of sensitive goods, contributing to the security and integrity of international trade transactions.

Topic 115: Procedure for air customs clearance

In navigating the procedures for clearing export goods through air customs, it's essential to recognize the parallels with sea transportation, albeit with specific adjustments tailored to air freight operations. While regulations and controls largely remain consistent regardless of the mode of transportation, the distinction lies in the customs' location and the practicalities involved in air cargo clearance.

Exporting goods via air demands adherence to a meticulous customs clearance process to ensure regulatory compliance and the smooth flow of export operations. Just as in sea transportation, air customs clearance entails a series of protocols and stages that exporters must diligently adhere to.

The first crucial step in the clearance procedure is compliance, which typically occurs before filing the shipping bill or export declaration. This involves obtaining the necessary export licenses, such as the Importer Exporter Code (IEC) number in India, from the local export administration, such as the Directorate General of Foreign Trade (DGFT). This prerequisite must be fulfilled prior to initiating the application for a shipping bill or export declaration.

In countries employing electronic filing systems like India's Electronic Data Interchange (EDI) or the United States' Automated Export System (AES), the issuance of the IEC number is seamlessly integrated into the customs' electronic platforms. Exporters are also often required to register locally with authorized foreign exchange dealers to facilitate the smooth processing of export proceeds, typically administered by central banks. This ensures compliance with foreign exchange control mechanisms, with exporters needing to obtain an Authorized Dealer (AD) number for transactions involving foreign currencies.

These initial compliance measures lay the foundation for subsequent steps in the air customs clearance process, setting the stage for efficient and regulatory-compliant export operations.

Continuing with the procedural intricacies of air customs clearance, exporters must also attend to additional requirements to streamline their operations effectively. Apart from securing the necessary licenses and registrations, establishing a designated business account with a commercial bank is imperative. In India, this often takes the form of a current account, serving as the conduit for receiving export incentives or reimbursements for duties paid on inputs.

Exporters participating in local export promotion schemes, aimed at incentivizing exports through various means, must ensure compliance with the requisite documentation. This may involve obtaining advance licenses or duty exemption entitlement certificates, tailored to specific export transactions. These documents, vital for availing export promotion benefits, must be registered with customs authorities at the relevant airport cargo terminals or air customs stations.

Failure to furnish the requisite licenses or permissions can impede the customs clearance process, hindering the seamless flow of export operations. Therefore, exporters must diligently adhere to these procedures to ensure regulatory compliance and capitalize on available export promotion incentives. By proactively fulfilling these requirements, exporters can navigate air customs clearance with efficiency and precision, fostering the smooth facilitation of international trade.

Topic 116: Processing of shipping bill - Non Electronic Processing

In cases where air customs operate through manual systems rather than electronic platforms, exporters must adhere to specific procedures for filing shipping bills or export declarations. These documents serve as crucial evidence of export and are filed in accordance with regulations outlined by the shipping bill and bill of export regulations of the respective country, such as India's 1991 regulation.

Exporters are required to obtain the prescribed format for shipping bills or bill of export, ensuring compliance with the specified guidelines. These formats, akin to export declarations, vary based on the nature of the goods being exported, distinguishing between duty-free, dutiable, or drawback goods. For instance, goods eligible for duty drawback schemes necessitate a separate entry in the shipping bill.

When filing shipping bill applications, exporters must submit all original documents, including invoices, packing lists, and any relevant forms, to air customs. While electronic filing may not immediately require these documents, they are crucial for manual processing. The Assessing Officer in the Export Department of Air Customs meticulously evaluates various aspects, including the value of goods, classification under drawback schedules, and eligibility under foreign trade policies.

In instances involving export promotion schemes, such as DEEC (Duty and Development Exemption Certificate) in India, specialized departments within customs, like the DEEC department, handle processing. These departments scrutinize EP (Export Promotion) shipping bills with heightened diligence due to the financial incentives or considerations involved. Assessing Officers verify that the description of goods matches the details specified in the relevant licenses or certificates, requesting samples for further inspection if necessary.

EP shipping bills undergo thorough scrutiny to ensure accuracy and compliance, given the monetary implications associated with government incentives or drawbacks. This meticulous approach underscores the importance of adhering to regulatory requirements and accurately documenting export transactions to facilitate smooth customs clearance processes.

In scenarios where shipping bills or bill of exports are not part of the electronic system, known as non-EDI shipping bills in India, specific procedures are followed to ensure compliance and smooth processing. Once the shipping bill receives approval from the Export Department of Customs, the exporter or their agent presents the goods to the supervisor of the shed, typically located in the holding or examination area at the airport.

In this examination area, a customs official, often referred to as the shed appraiser, supervises the examination of goods, which is usually conducted randomly. If necessary, the shed appraiser may delegate the examination to a customs officer, the actual examiner. Upon verifying that the description and particulars of the goods align with the declaration, the appraiser issues a crucial LET EXPORT order, signifying clearance for export.

After obtaining the LET EXPORT order, the exporter engages the preventive superintendent or relevant customs personnel to oversee the loading of goods onto the aircraft. This step ensures adherence to customs regulations and facilitates the smooth transition of goods for export.

However, if discrepancies are detected during examination, such as inconsistencies in goods or documentation, the examination staff may return the shipping bill to the export department with their observations. The export department then reevaluates the case, determining whether amendments to the description or value of goods are necessary before export can proceed. Additionally, actions under the Customs Act of 1962 may be initiated for any misdeclarations or discrepancies identified.

Ultimately, the issuance of the LET EXPORT order signifies the culmination of thorough examination and compliance checks, ensuring that goods are cleared for export in accordance with regulatory requirements.

Topic 117: Processing of shipping bill - Electronic processing

Under the Electronic Data Interchange (EDI) system, the processing of shipping bills becomes more streamlined and efficient. Export declarations are filed in the prescribed format through electronic means, typically facilitated by freight forwarders, shipping agents, or service centers designated by the customs department. This electronic filing is not directly accessible to exporters due to the sensitive nature of the process.

The exporter provides necessary details to the service center operator, who then enters the data into the customs department's EDI system. Upon verification of the provided information, the system generates a unique shipping bill number, essential for all subsequent procedures. This number is endorsed on a printed checklist provided by the service center operator and returned to the exporter for reference.

For export items subject to taxes or cess, such as TR 6 Challan in India, a document is printed immediately after the submission of the shipping bill application. This document enables the exporter to pay the applicable taxes at designated banks or customs systems.

Notably, no copy of the shipping bill is provided to the exporter or their representative at this stage, as the shipping bill can only be generated after the export process is completed and confirmed by customs. In many cases, the EDI system processes shipping bills based on the declarations made by the exporter, with minimal human intervention. However, random checks and sample examinations ensure compliance and prevent fraudulent activities.

In instances where human intervention is necessary, customs officers may review shipping bills on-screen and request samples for verification of declared values or classification of goods. Exporters or their representatives can seek assistance at query counters, typically located within service centers, to address any queries raised by the customs department.

Effective communication and compliance with customs procedures are crucial to ensure timely clearance of shipping bills and smooth export operations.

Topic 118: Local taxes exemption

When it comes to handling GST, VAT, or other local taxes on exported goods, customs clearance plays a vital role. The process ensures that exporters benefit from tax exemptions seamlessly.

Since the shipping bill is only generated after receiving the LET EXPORT order from customs, exporters do not possess the signed original shipping bill until the end of the process. However, exporters can utilize the export invoice or the shipping bill number, along with any other acceptable document, to claim exemption from local taxes.

In the case of India, GST is predominantly applicable, along with occasional instances of octoroi. Exporters navigate this process by leveraging appropriate documentation that satisfies the requirements of local tax authorities, ensuring smooth tax exemption procedures.

Topic 119: Exchange control formalities waiver

In international trade, the exchange control formalities, often represented by documents like the GR form, play a crucial role in regulating foreign exchange inflows and outflows. However, certain exemptions and waivers exist, particularly for smaller shipments or specific types of exports.

Typically, when shipping bills are processed electronically (EDI filing), an exchange control copy is automatically generated by the system and forwarded to the central bank for monitoring foreign exchange flows. In India, for instance, this document is known as the GR form (Guarantee Remittance form).

Nevertheless, exemptions from this requirement are granted in certain scenarios. For instance, smaller shipments or exports valued below a specified threshold may be eligible for waiver from the GR form obligation. In India, this waiver applies to exports valued at less than USD 25,000 or gifts valued up to Indian rupees 500,000.

These waivers streamline the export process for smaller transactions, eliminating unnecessary paperwork and facilitating smoother trade operations.

Topic 120: Arrival of export goods in examination area

Upon arrival at the customs examination area or holding area, export goods undergo further processing to ensure compliance with regulatory requirements. This stage marks the entry of the goods into the designated area, whether it be the dock for sea shipments or the examination area for air customs.

The entry of export goods into the examination area is authorized based on the documentation provided, primarily the checklist generated by the Customs Department's service center operator. This checklist contains essential information, including the shipping bill number and other export declaration papers required for clearance.

Once authorized, the custodian stationed at the examination area endorses the quantity of goods received on the reverse side of the checklist or relevant document. This endorsement serves as a confirmation of the actual quantity of goods received and facilitates further processing by the customs department.

In essence, the arrival of export goods in the examination area involves a meticulous verification process to ensure accurate documentation and adherence to regulatory standards.

Topic 121: Customs examination of export goods

In the process of customs examination for export goods, meticulous verification ensures compliance with regulations. While not all shipments require examination, a percentage undergoes scrutiny to uphold standards.

Upon receipt of goods in the examination area, the exporter or their representative presents the endorsed checklist and original documents to the designated customs officer. These documents include the commercial invoice, packing list, and any other relevant forms.

The customs officer verifies the received quantity against the endorsed checklist, entering details into the electronic system, such as Icegate in India. Subsequently, the officer electronically marks the shipping bill and assigns a customs officer for examination, indicating the packages to be inspected.

Random packages, if any, are examined to ensure conformity with the provided documentation. The examination report is then entered into the EDI system, and the shipping bill, along with all original documents, is passed to the shed appraiser or dock appraiser for further processing.

If the shed appraiser confirms compliance with the descriptions in the original documents and the physical examination, they proceed to allow the LET EXPORT order. The exporter or CHA is notified via the service center, facilitating smooth clearance of the shipment.

Topic 122: Factory Stuffing Permission

In the export process, obtaining factory stuffing permission is a crucial step, allowing customs intervention at the factory itself. Most countries offer this facility, albeit subject to certain safeguards.

A single factory stuffing permission, valid across all customs stations, is typically granted instead of station-wise permissions. However, exporters must provide a list of customs stations they intend to use. This list enables customs to maintain records and assign a unique serial number to each permission.

The customs house granting the permission maintains a register for tracking and circulates the permission to all relevant customs houses. This includes details of the Preventive Officer, Inspector, Superintendent, and Central Excise range for verification purposes.

In case of any adverse findings against the exporter, the concerned customs station promptly informs the granting customs house. Subsequently, the permission is withdrawn, and all relevant customs houses are notified.

While the specifics may vary by country, this process ensures smooth coordination between exporters and customs authorities, facilitating efficient export operations.

Topic 123: Variation Between Declaration and Physical Examination

In the event of any variance between the declared information and the findings of a physical examination, customs authorities follow a specific protocol to address the discrepancy.

Upon detecting any inconsistency, the appraiser retains the checklist, declaration, and all original documents submitted with the shipping bill. If a variance is identified, the appraiser escalates the matter to the Assistant Commissioner or Deputy Commissioner of Customs (Exports), depending on the jurisdiction.

The exporter or their representative is then instructed to meet with the customs authority for resolving the dispute or addressing any deficiencies. If the exporter agrees with the customs department's assessment, the shipping bill is processed accordingly.

However, if the exporter disputes the department's findings, the matter is settled in accordance with the principles of natural justice. This standard procedure ensures fair resolution of discrepancies, promoting transparency and compliance with customs regulations across different countries.

Topic 124: Drawl of Samples

When samples are required to be drawn for testing or other purposes, customs authorities follow a systematic procedure to ensure accuracy and fairness.

Upon orders from the shed appraiser or dock appraiser, customs officers proceed to draw samples from the consignment. Typically, two samples are drawn, and their details, along with the testing agency information, are recorded in the customs' electronic system, such as Icegate in India.

Subsequently, three copies of the test memo are prepared, each signed by the customs officer, appraising officers, and the exporter or their representative (Customs House Agent - CHA). These copies serve different purposes:

The original copy is sent with the sample to the testing agency.

The duplicate copy, or customs copy, is retained with the second sample.

The triplicate copy is retained by the exporter as their record.

Additionally, if deemed necessary by higher customs authorities like the Assistant Commissioner or Deputy Commissioner of Customs, samples may be ordered for purposes other than testing. This could include visual inspection, verification of descriptions, market value inquiries, or any other relevant reasons.

This standardized process ensures transparency and adherence to customs regulations while conducting sample tests or inspections.

Topic 125: Loading of goods in ULD

The process of loading goods for air shipment involves careful coordination between exporters, airline agents, and customs authorities, especially when utilizing Unit Load Devices (ULDs).

To initiate the loading process, the exporter or their agent must provide the exporter's copy of the shipping bill, duly signed by the shed appraiser or examination area appraiser, indicating the LET EXPORT order. This document is then handed over to the airline's agent, who seeks approval from the customs preventive officer for loading the shipment into ULD containers.

The stuffing of ULD containers at the cargo airport is conducted under the preventive supervision of customs officers, ensuring compliance with regulations and security measures. The customs preventive superintendent at the docks or shed enters specific details into the customs' electronic system, such as Icegate in India, including the seal number and loading particulars of the ULD onto the aircraft.

If any discrepancies arise, such as differences in the quantity or number of packages loaded, the superintendent may note these on the shipping bill in the EDI system, signaling the need for amendments. Until these discrepancies are rectified, the shipping bill may not be processed for sanction of drawbacks or incentives.

Once the loading process is completed, the customs preventive officer overseeing the operation provides a "shipped on board" endorsement on the exporter's copy of the shipping bill, confirming the goods' inclusion in the shipment.

This meticulous process, overseen by customs authorities, ensures the efficient and secure loading of goods into ULD containers for air transport, maintaining compliance with international shipping standards.

Topic 126: Amendments

In the export process, amendments may be necessary to correct errors or update information in the shipping documentation. The procedures for amendments vary depending on the stage of the export process and the status of the shipping bill.

If corrections are required before the shipping bill number is generated and documents are submitted in the EDI system, amendments can be made at the service center. However, once the shipping bill number is generated or the goods are brought into the export examination area, amendments follow a different process.

There are typically two scenarios for amendments:

If the goods have not yet received LET EXPORT order, amendments require approval from a senior customs official, such as the Assistant Commissioner of the Exports Department.

If LET EXPORT order has been granted, amendments require approval from an even higher-ranking customs official, such as the Additional or Joint Commissioner of Customs.

After obtaining permission for amendments, the Assistant Commissioner or Deputy Commissioner of Exports may approve the changes in the EDI system, representing the higher-ranking customs official. If the shipping bill has already been generated, the exporter must surrender all copies to the dock or shed appraiser for cancellation before amendments can be approved in the EDI system.

These procedures ensure that amendments are conducted accurately and in compliance with customs regulations, facilitating smooth processing of export shipments.

Topic 127: Drawback Claim

In the process of exporting goods, drawback claims play a significant role in facilitating reimbursements to exporters for certain duties or taxes paid on the exported products. Here's a closer look at how the drawback claim process unfolds in air customs:

Automatic Processing: After the actual export of goods, drawback claims are automatically processed through the Electronic Data Interchange (EDI) systems by officers of the drawback branch. This is done on a first come, first served basis.

Query Resolution: The status of shipping bills and the sanction of drawback claims can be checked at the query counter set up at the service center, as mentioned earlier. Any queries or deficiencies noticed in the system are displayed on the terminal of the service center operator. Authorized personnel of the exporter or the exporter themselves can obtain a printout of these queries from the service center query counter.

Response to Queries: Exporters are required to respond to these queries either through the service center or directly from the terminal of the Customs House Agent (CHA), if authorized. It's essential to address these queries promptly to ensure smooth processing.

Transfer and Crediting: Once claims are sanctioned, they are transferred to the bank through the online system. The bank then credits the drawback amount directly into the respective exporter's accounts.

Confirmation of Export: To enable customs to sanction the drawback claim, the airline electronically transfers the Export General Manifest (EGM) to the customs EDI system. This confirms and verifies the physical export of goods. Without this EGM, customs cannot sanction the drawback claims.

By following these steps, exporters can efficiently claim drawbacks on their exported goods, contributing to smoother transactions and financial reimbursements.

Topic 128: Generation of Shipping Bills & EGM

In the final stages of the export process, the generation of shipping bills and Export General Manifest (EGM) takes place, marking the culmination of the customs clearance procedures. Here's a closer look at how this process unfolds:

Shipping Bill Generation: Shipping bills are generated only after the LET EXPORT order is issued by the appraiser on the Electronic Data Interchange (EDI) system. The shipping bill is generated in two copies: the customs copy and the exporter's copy (EP copy). The EP copy is generated after the submission of the EGM, which is transferred by the airline.

Signatures and Documentation: Upon obtaining the printout, the appraiser secures signatures of the customs officer and the representative of the Customs House Agent (CHA) or the CHA itself on both copies of the shipping bill and the examination report. The customs copy, along with the original declarations, is retained by the appraiser and forwarded to the Export Department of the CHA, while the exporter's copy is returned to the exporter or their agent.

Exchange Control Copy: Simultaneously, the exchange control copy of the shipping bill is sent to the central bank, ensuring compliance with exchange control regulations.

Export General Manifest (EGM) Submission: Airlines are required to furnish the EGM, shipping bill-wise, to customs electronically before the departure of the flight. Additionally, manual EGMs, along with the exporter's copy of the shipping bills, are submitted to the Export Department of customs for processing. These manual submissions may be entered into a register or logged into the EDI system, depending on the customs procedures.

Acknowledgment and Record-Keeping: Upon submission of the EGMs, airlines obtain acknowledgments indicating the date and time of receipt by the Export Department of customs. This facilitates proper record-keeping and ensures compliance with regulatory requirements.

While minor differences may exist in customs procedures across different countries, the overarching process remains consistent, ensuring the smooth and efficient generation of shipping bills and EGMs to facilitate international trade transactions.

Topic 129: Air transportation industry

When it comes to transporting goods swiftly and efficiently, air transportation emerges as the preferred choice for various categories of items, including time-sensitive goods, documents, and high-value items. The key advantages of air shipment lie in its speed and convenience, making it indispensable for businesses worldwide.

In the air transportation industry, there are primarily two types of air cargo carriers:

Dedicated Cargo Carriers: These carriers operate specifically for cargo transportation, utilizing wide-bodied aircraft with tall fuselage cross-sections. This design allows for the transportation of voluminous goods, making them ideal for various cargo types. Dedicated cargo aircraft often feature a high wing configuration, enabling the cargo area to sit close to the ground for easy loading and unloading. Additionally, they are equipped with numerous wheels to facilitate landing at unprepared locations or difficult airstrips. One notable feature is the high-mounted tail, which enables direct loading and unloading of cargo.

Cargo Division of Commercial Passenger Airlines: Commercial passenger airlines also offer cargo transportation services, utilizing the cargo hold in passenger aircraft. These airlines utilize leftover spaces in the belly of passenger aircraft for commercial cargo transportation, making efficient use of available capacity.

In terms of usage, data from 2015 indicates that 43% of internationally moved goods, amounting to 700 billion ATK, were served by dedicated freighters, while 57% utilized cargo holds. However, by 2035, it is projected that 37% of goods, totaling 1200 B ATK, would be served by dedicated freighters, with 63% utilizing cargo holds. This reflects the increasing popularity of utilizing cargo holds for commercial cargo movement by international airlines.

In terms of aircraft classification, there are generally four types:

Derivatives of Non-Cargo Aircraft: These aircraft are adapted from existing models to accommodate cargo transportation needs. They are versatile and can transport various types of goods, including general and specialized cargo, utilizing containers or Unit Load Devices (ULDs).

Dedicated Civilian Cargo Aircraft: These aircraft are specifically designed for civilian cargo transport, offering efficient and reliable services for businesses across the globe.

Joint Civil and Military Cargo Aircraft: Some aircraft serve both civilian and military purposes, facilitating cargo transport on national and international routes.

Unpiloted Cargo Aircraft (Drones): With advancements in technology, unpiloted cargo aircraft, commonly known as drones, have emerged as a viable option for cargo transportation, offering innovative solutions for logistics management.

These aircraft provide diverse options for cargo moving agencies and organizations involved in international logistics management, catering to different requirements and preferences.

In India, numerous major airports serve as crucial hubs for air cargo operations. These airports, including those in New Delhi, Mumbai, Chennai, and Bangalore, are equipped with modern facilities to handle various types of air cargo efficiently. Similarly, major airports worldwide play significant roles in facilitating air cargo movements, with rankings and listings available to assess their capabilities and facilities.

Regulations imposed by organizations such as the International Air Transport Association (IATA) are crucial for ensuring safety and compliance in air cargo transportation, particularly concerning the transportation of dangerous or hazardous goods. These regulations dictate packing requirements, documentation procedures, handling protocols, and associated costs, ensuring the safe and secure transportation of goods by air.

Understanding and adhering to international regulations is essential for all stakeholders in the air cargo industry to maintain safety standards and ensure the smooth operation of air cargo services worldwide. Organizations like the International Air Transport Association (IATA) and the International Civil Aviation Organization (ICAO) set guidelines and regulations that govern various aspects of air cargo transportation. For example, IATA regulations focus on the transportation of dangerous or hazardous goods, dictating packing requirements, documentation procedures, and handling protocols.

ICAO regulations cover a broader spectrum, including safety, security, environmental protection, and international agreements and conventions. These regulations, such as the Warsaw Convention of 1929, apply universally to air cargo movements, ensuring standardized practices and procedures across the industry. Additionally, each country may have its own local regulations, such as the Carriage of Goods by Air Act of 1972 in India, which shippers and carriers must comply with.

When examining the air cargo industry, several key characteristics emerge:

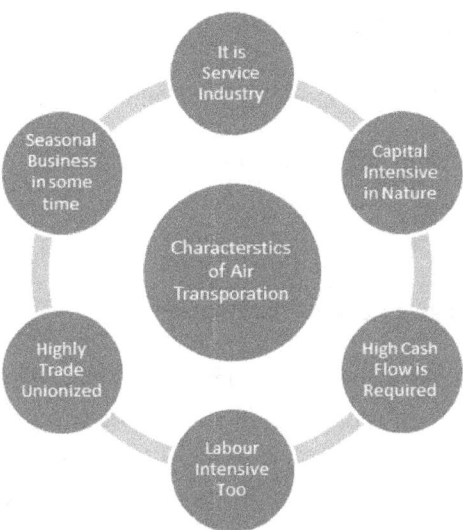

Service-Centric Nature: The air cargo industry revolves around providing efficient and timely services, making it a service-centric sector.

Capital Intensive: The industry requires significant capital investment to establish and operate, given the high costs associated with infrastructure, equipment, and technology.

Labor Intensive: Skilled and semi-skilled labor plays a crucial role in various aspects of air cargo operations, contributing to the industry's labor-intensive nature.

Trade Unionization: Air transportation is often heavily unionized in many countries, with organized labor groups advocating for the rights and interests of workers.

Seasonal Business: The demand for air cargo transportation fluctuates seasonally and varies across different regions and zones, leading to fluctuations in business activity throughout the year.

Understanding these characteristics is essential for stakeholders in the air transportation industry to navigate its complexities and operate successfully in a dynamic and competitive environment.

Topic 130: Frequently Asked Questions (FAQs) - Export by Air:

What is the maximum crate size for air freight?

The largest dimension allowable on a wide-bodied passenger aircraft is typically 310 centimeters in length, 240 centimeters in width, and 160 centimeters in height.

How do you arrange air cargo shipments?

To ship your package via air cargo, simply contact a reputable air cargo shipping service. Their representative will guide you through the process and manage the logistics for your shipment. It's important to understand the process to negotiate and instruct properly, as your goods and reputation are at stake.

What items are generally prohibited in air cargo?

Items prohibited in air cargo include dangerous goods listed by the United Nations, such as lithium batteries, power banks, firearms, flammable substances, explosives, and certain chemicals. The United Nations provides a complete list of such goods and their associated danger levels.

Is air freight more expensive than sea freight?

Yes, air freight is considerably more expensive than sea freight. The rapid delivery offered by air cargo comes at a higher cost compared to the slower but more economical sea transportation.

How does air freight differ from ocean freight?

Air freight is notably faster in transportation, while ocean freight tends to be slower but more cost-effective. Although the bulk of international trade still occurs via sea transportation, the significance of air freight is increasing due to its speed. Aircraft can handle smaller quantities of cargo compared to ocean freight, which has larger capacities.

What distinguishes air cargo from air freight?

The terms "air cargo" and "air freight" are often used interchangeably. However, air cargo typically refers to goods transported by a third-party carrier on a plane, while air freight may encompass both third-party transportation and freight companies moving cargo on their own planes for proprietary use. The distinction may vary depending on specific logistics companies.

Topic 131: Section take away

In this section, we delved into the intricate process of exporting goods by air, providing comprehensive insights into various aspects of air freight shipments. We discussed the nuances of air freight, comparing it with other modes of transportation such as road and sea shipment. Furthermore, we outlined the essential documents required for air cargo exports, emphasizing their significance in facilitating smooth transactions.

Throughout our discussion, we shed light on the role of customs authorities and the meticulous scrutiny involved in clearing export goods. From the initial documentation to the loading of goods onto aircraft, we explored each step of the process in detail, aiming to provide you with a comprehensive understanding of air cargo exports.

By familiarizing yourself with the procedures outlined in this section, you now possess a solid foundation for navigating the complexities of air freight shipments in your export business. While we primarily focused on examples from Indian customs, the principles discussed here are applicable across various countries with similar customs systems.

As you continue your export journey, I encourage you to delve deeper into the specific requirements and regulations governing air cargo exports in your country. By conducting further research and seeking clarification on any differences or nuances, you can ensure compliance with local regulations and optimize your export operations.

With this knowledge at your disposal, you are well-equipped to navigate the intricacies of air cargo exports and propel your business towards greater success in the global market.

Chapter 16: INCOTERMS 2020 Rules

Topic 132: Chapter Overview

Welcome back to our book. Today, we delve into a crucial aspect of international trade - the International Commercial Terms, commonly known as INCOTERMS. These terms play a pivotal role in international sales contracts and the management of export shipments' logistics.

In this lecture, our focus is on understanding the intricacies of INCOTERMS 2020. These terms delineate the obligations and risks associated with international transactions, including the allocation of costs, responsibilities for transportation, loading, unloading, and incidental expenses.

It's essential to grasp the distinction between the points at which the seller's obligations transfer to the importer and when the risk shifts from the seller to the importer. These points may not always align, adding a layer of complexity to international trade agreements.

As of January 2020, the International Chamber of Commerce (ICC) in

Paris, France, has introduced the latest set of INCOTERMS - the Incoterms 2020. These terms consist of 11 distinct clauses, each specifying different aspects of the transaction process.

Throughout this lecture, I will elucidate these INCOTERMS 2020 clauses, elucidating the points of obligation transfer and risk allocation between buyers and sellers. By the end, you'll gain a comprehensive understanding of these crucial terms, empowering you to navigate international trade transactions with confidence.

Let's delve into the intricacies of INCOTERMS 2020 and unravel their significance in global commerce.

Topic 133: Understanding INCOTERMS 2020

In the realm of international trade, comprehending the movement of goods from exporter to importer is paramount. As depicted in the diagram, this journey begins at the exporter's warehouse, where goods are loaded onto the first carrier, typically a truck or lorry. Subsequently, the goods are transported to the port of loading, where they are transferred onto a ship for transit to the port of discharge.

Upon arrival at the port of discharge, the goods undergo unloading and are then loaded onto another truck or lorry for transportation to the agreed delivery location, which may be the importer's warehouse or another specified destination. Throughout this process, various zones are traversed, including the exporter's warehouse, the port of loading, the high seas during maritime transit, and the port of discharge.

It's essential to recognize these distinct zones, as they delineate crucial points where the transfer of obligations and risks between the seller and the buyer may occur. The agreed delivery location marks the endpoint of this journey, where the goods are ultimately received by the buyer.

Understanding these zones and the associated shifts in obligations and risks is fundamental to effectively applying the principles outlined in the

INCOTERMS 2020 rules. These rules serve as a guiding framework for international sales contracts, clarifying the responsibilities and liabilities of both parties involved in the transaction.

By grasping the nuances of these zones and their implications within the context of international trade, one can navigate the complexities of global commerce with clarity and confidence.

Topic 134: E, F and C INCOTERMS 2020

In the realm of international trade, understanding the intricacies of INCOTERMS 2020 is essential for effectively navigating the complexities of global commerce. These terms delineate the points at which obligations and risks shift between the seller and the buyer throughout the transportation process.

Beginning with the exporter's warehouse, the EXW (Ex Works) term signifies that the seller fulfills their obligations upon delivering the goods at the specified location. Moving to the agreed place in the exporter's country, represented in green, the FCA (Free Carrier) term denotes the transfer of both obligations and risks to the buyer upon loading the goods onto the first carrier.

If the seller is responsible for paying the freight cost to the agreed place, the term is CPT (Carriage Paid To), while CIP (Carriage and Insurance Paid To) includes insurance coverage up to the agreed place. Despite the transfer of obligations, the risk is already assumed by the buyer upon loading the goods onto the first carrier.

Transitioning to the port of loading, where the ship takes berth, sea terms such as FOB (Free on Board) signify that both obligations and risks transfer to the buyer upon loading the goods onto the ship. Alternatively, FAS (Free Alongside Ship) places the responsibility of loading on the buyer, reducing costs and risks for the seller.

These INCOTERMS 2020 provide a structured framework for international sales contracts, clarifying the responsibilities and liabilities of both parties involved in the transaction. By understanding these terms and their implications, businesses can facilitate smoother transactions and mitigate risks in the global marketplace.

Continuing our exploration of INCOTERMS 2020, let's delve into the C terms, specifically CFR and CIF.

CFR (Cost and Freight) mirrors FOB in many aspects. However, in CFR, it is the seller's responsibility to not only load the goods onto the ship but also cover the freight cost for carriage to the port of discharge. Despite this obligation, the risk is already transferred to the buyer at the port of loading.

Moving forward, CIF (Cost, Insurance, and Freight) encompasses similar responsibilities to CFR. In CIF, the seller is obligated to load the goods onto the ship, cover the freight cost, and additionally provide insurance coverage for the main carriage from the port of loading to the port of discharge. Like CFR, the risk shifts to the buyer at the port of loading.

These C terms play a crucial role in international trade contracts, offering clarity on the division of responsibilities and liabilities between the seller and the buyer. Depending on the nature of the goods, the logistics involved, and other specific requirements, these terms are flexibly utilized to ensure smooth transactions and mitigate risks in the global marketplace.

Topic 135: D terms

In our exploration of INCOTERMS 2020, we now shift our focus to the D terms, which encompass the green zone in the importer's country. There are two key D terms: DPU and DAP.

DAP, or Delivered at Place, entails the seller bearing both the obligation and risk until the agreed place in the importer's country. However, the goods are loaded onto the buyer's truck, shifting the responsibility for unloading and any associated charges to the buyer.

Similarly, DPU, or Delivered at Place Unloaded, shares the same obligations and risks as DAP but includes the additional responsibility of unloading the goods by the seller.

Lastly, DDP, or Delivered Duty Paid, marks the final destination in the importer's country—the importer's warehouse. Here, the seller assumes full responsibility, including unloading, and is tasked with clearing the goods through customs, paying any duties, taxes, or fees required for importation.

Understanding these D terms is paramount for negotiating international purchase contracts, ensuring clarity and accountability between parties involved in global trade transactions.

Topic 136: Summary of all 11 INCOTERMS 2020

In our discussion of INCOTERMS 2020, we have explored the intricacies of international trade agreements, defining the responsibilities and risks associated with each stage of the journey from seller to buyer. Here's a summary of all 11 INCOTERMS:

EXW (Ex Works): The seller's obligation ends at their premises, and the buyer assumes all risks and costs from that point.

FCA (Free Carrier): The seller delivers the goods to the carrier at a specified location, transferring risk to the buyer upon delivery to the carrier.

FAS (Free Alongside Ship): The seller delivers the goods alongside the vessel at a specified port, with risk transferring to the buyer at that point.

FOB (Free on Board): The seller is responsible for delivering the goods on board the vessel at the specified port, with risk transferring to the buyer once the goods are on board.

CFR (Cost and Freight): The seller pays for transportation to the specified port of destination, with risk transferring to the buyer once the goods are on board the vessel.

CIF (Cost, Insurance, and Freight): Similar to CFR, but the seller also arranges insurance, with risk transferring to the buyer once the goods are on board the vessel.

CPT (Carriage Paid To): The seller pays for transportation to the specified destination, with risk transferring to the buyer upon delivery to the carrier.

CIP (Carriage and Insurance Paid To): Similar to CPT, but the seller also arranges insurance, with risk transferring to the buyer upon delivery to the carrier.

DPU (Delivered at Place Unloaded): The seller delivers the goods to the specified destination and unloads them, assuming all risks and costs until delivery.

DAP (Delivered at Place): Similar to DPU, but the seller is not responsible for unloading the goods.

DDP (Delivered Duty Paid): The seller is responsible for delivering the goods to the specified destination, including customs clearance and payment of all duties and taxes, assuming all risks and costs until delivery.

Understanding these INCOTERMS is essential for effectively negotiating international trade contracts and ensuring clarity and accountability throughout the shipping process.

Book Conclusion

Congratulations on completing this comprehensive book on international logistics management! I want to extend my heartfelt thanks to each and every one of you for your dedication and commitment throughout this journey.

But wait, our journey doesn't end here. I'm continuously working to enhance this book with new topics, resources, and bonus sections. So, I encourage you to keep revisiting the book to stay updated on the latest information and resources that will be added over time.

Throughout this book, you've gained a solid understanding of the fundamental concepts of international logistics management, including the various modes of transportation for goods. This knowledge equips you to make informed business decisions regarding the movement of goods across borders and fosters stronger relationships with your international partners.

If you found the content valuable and beneficial, I encourage you to share this book with your colleagues and friends who may also benefit from it. Additionally, I kindly request you to take a moment to rate this book and provide your positive feedback. Your input is incredibly valuable and helps me tailor future updates to better meet your needs.

Once again, thank you for your participation and dedication to learning. I look forward to seeing you revisit the book and continue your journey in mastering international logistics management.

ABOUT THE AUTHOR

Dr. Vijesh Jain is *a corporate trainer, management consultant, and instructor of* VJ Export Mastery Courses Series on UDEMY. He has written more than 10 books on export and import related topics. These books are available on Amazom and Kindle. He already has more than a quarter million of student enrollments on Udemy. He is an MIB, IIFT, New Delhi, B.E.BITS, Pilani, Phd from University of Mysore and a Certified Global Business Professional by NASBITE, USA. He is the first ever recipient of the best PhD thesis award conferred by BIMTECH, Delhi NCR. He has also contributed several research papers, those are published in top international research journals. He is the pioneer research scientist in the area of cross cultural management research, having postulated CFC dimension of world cultures. He is widely travelled abroad, having worked with top multinational companies involved in global business and has attended several international conferences and presented papers there. He has trained 1000s of working executives in India and abroad in the area of Global Management, Foreign Trade, Blockchain and Metaverse applications in international trade operations. With a total work experience of more than 35 years with global companies, he has also worked as Dean/Director with several reputed B Schools.